C-2168 CAREER EXAMINATION SERIES

This is your
PASSBOOK for...

Systems Analyst

Test Preparation Study Guide
Questions & Answers

COPYRIGHT NOTICE

This book is SOLELY intended for, is sold ONLY to, and its use is RESTRICTED to individual, bona fide applicants or candidates who qualify by virtue of having seriously filed applications for appropriate license, certificate, professional and/or promotional advancement, higher school matriculation, scholarship, or other legitimate requirements of education and/or governmental authorities.

This book is NOT intended for use, class instruction, tutoring, training, duplication, copying, reprinting, excerption, or adaptation, etc., by:

1) Other publishers
2) Proprietors and/or Instructors of "Coaching" and/or Preparatory Courses
3) Personnel and/or Training Divisions of commercial, industrial, and governmental organizations
4) Schools, colleges, or universities and/or their departments and staffs, including teachers and other personnel
5) Testing Agencies or Bureaus
6) Study groups which seek by the purchase of a single volume to copy and/or duplicate and/or adapt this material for use by the group as a whole without having purchased individual volumes for each of the members of the group
7) Et al.

Such persons would be in violation of appropriate Federal and State statutes.

PROVISION OF LICENSING AGREEMENTS – Recognized educational, commercial, industrial, and governmental institutions and organizations, and others legitimately engaged in educational pursuits, including training, testing, and measurement activities, may address request for a licensing agreement to the copyright owners, who will determine whether, and under what conditions, including fees and charges, the materials in this book may be used them. In other words, a licensing facility exists for the legitimate use of the material in this book on other than an individual basis. However, it is asseverated and affirmed here that the material in this book CANNOT be used without the receipt of the express permission of such a licensing agreement from the Publishers. Inquiries re licensing should be addressed to the company, attention rights and permissions department.

All rights reserved, including the right of reproduction in whole or in part, in any form or by any means, electronic or mechanical, including photocopying, recording, or by any information storage and retrieval system, without permission in writing from the Publisher.

Copyright © 2025 by
National Learning Corporation

212 Michael Drive, Syosset, NY 11791
(516) 921-8888 • www.passbooks.com
E-mail: info@passbooks.com

PASSBOOK® SERIES

THE *PASSBOOK® SERIES* has been created to prepare applicants and candidates for the ultimate academic battlefield – the examination room.

At some time in our lives, each and every one of us may be required to take an examination – for validation, matriculation, admission, qualification, registration, certification, or licensure.

Based on the assumption that every applicant or candidate has met the basic formal educational standards, has taken the required number of courses, and read the necessary texts, the *PASSBOOK® SERIES* furnishes the one special preparation which may assure passing with confidence, instead of failing with insecurity. Examination questions – together with answers – are furnished as the basic vehicle for study so that the mysteries of the examination and its compounding difficulties may be eliminated or diminished by a sure method.

This book is meant to help you pass your examination provided that you qualify and are serious in your objective.

The entire field is reviewed through the huge store of content information which is succinctly presented through a provocative and challenging approach – the question-and-answer method.

A climate of success is established by furnishing the correct answers at the end of each test.

You soon learn to recognize types of questions, forms of questions, and patterns of questioning. You may even begin to anticipate expected outcomes.

You perceive that many questions are repeated or adapted so that you can gain acute insights, which may enable you to score many sure points.

You learn how to confront new questions, or types of questions, and to attack them confidently and work out the correct answers.

You note objectives and emphases, and recognize pitfalls and dangers, so that you may make positive educational adjustments.

Moreover, you are kept fully informed in relation to new concepts, methods, practices, and directions in the field.

You discover that you are actually taking the examination all the time: you are preparing for the examination by "taking" an examination, not by reading extraneous and/or supererogatory textbooks.

In short, this PASSBOOK®, used directedly, should be an important factor in helping you to pass your test.

SYSTEMS ANALYST

DUTIES
Performs complex technical and supervisory duties involving programming, systems and departmental procedure analysis. Surveys and analyzes work methods and procedures in order to formulate data processing systems; performs related work as required.

SCOPE OF THE EXAMINATION
The written test will cover knowledge, skills and/or abilities in such areas as:

1. Data processing concepts and terminology;
2. Systems analysis;
3. Symbolic logic;
4. Supervision; and
5. Preparing written material.

HOW TO TAKE A TEST

I. YOU MUST PASS AN EXAMINATION

A. WHAT EVERY CANDIDATE SHOULD KNOW

Examination applicants often ask us for help in preparing for the written test. What can I study in advance? What kinds of questions will be asked? How will the test be given? How will the papers be graded?

As an applicant for a civil service examination, you may be wondering about some of these things. Our purpose here is to suggest effective methods of advance study and to describe civil service examinations.

Your chances for success on this examination can be increased if you know how to prepare. Those "pre-examination jitters" can be reduced if you know what to expect. You can even experience an adventure in good citizenship if you know why civil service exams are given.

B. WHY ARE CIVIL SERVICE EXAMINATIONS GIVEN?

Civil service examinations are important to you in two ways. As a citizen, you want public jobs filled by employees who know how to do their work. As a job seeker, you want a fair chance to compete for that job on an equal footing with other candidates. The best-known means of accomplishing this two-fold goal is the competitive examination.

Exams are widely publicized throughout the nation. They may be administered for jobs in federal, state, city, municipal, town or village governments or agencies.

Any citizen may apply, with some limitations, such as the age or residence of applicants. Your experience and education may be reviewed to see whether you meet the requirements for the particular examination. When these requirements exist, they are reasonable and applied consistently to all applicants. Thus, a competitive examination may cause you some uneasiness now, but it is your privilege and safeguard.

C. HOW ARE CIVIL SERVICE EXAMS DEVELOPED?

Examinations are carefully written by trained technicians who are specialists in the field known as "psychological measurement," in consultation with recognized authorities in the field of work that the test will cover. These experts recommend the subject matter areas or skills to be tested; only those knowledges or skills important to your success on the job are included. The most reliable books and source materials available are used as references. Together, the experts and technicians judge the difficulty level of the questions.

Test technicians know how to phrase questions so that the problem is clearly stated. Their ethics do not permit "trick" or "catch" questions. Questions may have been tried out on sample groups, or subjected to statistical analysis, to determine their usefulness.

Written tests are often used in combination with performance tests, ratings of training and experience, and oral interviews. All of these measures combine to form the best-known means of finding the right person for the right job.

II. HOW TO PASS THE WRITTEN TEST

A. NATURE OF THE EXAMINATION

To prepare intelligently for civil service examinations, you should know how they differ from school examinations you have taken. In school you were assigned certain definite pages to read or subjects to cover. The examination questions were quite detailed and usually emphasized memory. Civil service exams, on the other hand, try to discover your present ability to perform the duties of a position, plus your potentiality to learn these duties. In other words, a civil service exam attempts to predict how successful you will be. Questions cover such a broad area that they cannot be as minute and detailed as school exam questions.

In the public service similar kinds of work, or positions, are grouped together in one "class." This process is known as *position-classification*. All the positions in a class are paid according to the salary range for that class. One class title covers all of these positions, and they are all tested by the same examination.

B. FOUR BASIC STEPS

1) Study the announcement

How, then, can you know what subjects to study? Our best answer is: "Learn as much as possible about the class of positions for which you've applied." The exam will test the knowledge, skills and abilities needed to do the work.

Your most valuable source of information about the position you want is the official exam announcement. This announcement lists the training and experience qualifications. Check these standards and apply only if you come reasonably close to meeting them.

The brief description of the position in the examination announcement offers some clues to the subjects which will be tested. Think about the job itself. Review the duties in your mind. Can you perform them, or are there some in which you are rusty? Fill in the blank spots in your preparation.

Many jurisdictions preview the written test in the exam announcement by including a section called "Knowledge and Abilities Required," "Scope of the Examination," or some similar heading. Here you will find out specifically what fields will be tested.

2) Review your own background

Once you learn in general what the position is all about, and what you need to know to do the work, ask yourself which subjects you already know fairly well and which need improvement. You may wonder whether to concentrate on improving your strong areas or on building some background in your fields of weakness. When the announcement has specified "some knowledge" or "considerable knowledge," or has used adjectives like "beginning principles of..." or "advanced ... methods," you can get a clue as to the number and difficulty of questions to be asked in any given field. More questions, and hence broader coverage, would be included for those subjects which are more important in the work. Now weigh your strengths and weaknesses against the job requirements and prepare accordingly.

3) Determine the level of the position

Another way to tell how intensively you should prepare is to understand the level of the job for which you are applying. Is it the entering level? In other words, is this the position in which beginners in a field of work are hired? Or is it an intermediate or advanced level? Sometimes this is indicated by such words as "Junior" or "Senior" in the class title. Other jurisdictions use Roman numerals to designate the level – Clerk I, Clerk II, for example. The word "Supervisor" sometimes appears in the title. If the level is not indicated by the title, check the description of duties. Will you be working under very close supervision, or will you have responsibility for independent decisions in this work?

4) Choose appropriate study materials

Now that you know the subjects to be examined and the relative amount of each subject to be covered, you can choose suitable study materials. For beginning level jobs, or even advanced ones, if you have a pronounced weakness in some aspect of your training, read a modern, standard textbook in that field. Be sure it is up to date and has general coverage. Such books are normally available at your library, and the librarian will be glad to help you locate one. For entry-level positions, questions of appropriate difficulty are chosen – neither highly advanced questions, nor those too simple. Such questions require careful thought but not advanced training.

If the position for which you are applying is technical or advanced, you will read more advanced, specialized material. If you are already familiar with the basic principles of your field, elementary textbooks would waste your time. Concentrate on advanced textbooks and technical periodicals. Think through the concepts and review difficult problems in your field.

These are all general sources. You can get more ideas on your own initiative, following these leads. For example, training manuals and publications of the government agency which employs workers in your field can be useful, particularly for technical and professional positions. A letter or visit to the government department involved may result in more specific study suggestions, and certainly will provide you with a more definite idea of the exact nature of the position you are seeking.

III. KINDS OF TESTS

Tests are used for purposes other than measuring knowledge and ability to perform specified duties. For some positions, it is equally important to test ability to make adjustments to new situations or to profit from training. In others, basic mental abilities not dependent on information are essential. Questions which test these things may not appear as pertinent to the duties of the position as those which test for knowledge and information. Yet they are often highly important parts of a fair examination. For very general questions, it is almost impossible to help you direct your study efforts. What we can do is to point out some of the more common of these general abilities needed in public service positions and describe some typical questions.

1) General information

Broad, general information has been found useful for predicting job success in some kinds of work. This is tested in a variety of ways, from vocabulary lists to questions about current events. Basic background in some field of work, such as sociology or economics, may be sampled in a group of questions. Often these are principles which have become familiar to most persons through exposure rather than through formal training. It is difficult to advise you how to study for these questions; being alert to the world around you is our best suggestion.

2) Verbal ability

An example of an ability needed in many positions is verbal or language ability. Verbal ability is, in brief, the ability to use and understand words. Vocabulary and grammar tests are typical measures of this ability. Reading comprehension or paragraph interpretation questions are common in many kinds of civil service tests. You are given a paragraph of written material and asked to find its central meaning.

3) Numerical ability

Number skills can be tested by the familiar arithmetic problem, by checking paired lists of numbers to see which are alike and which are different, or by interpreting charts and graphs. In the latter test, a graph may be printed in the test booklet which you are asked to use as the basis for answering questions.

4) Observation

A popular test for law-enforcement positions is the observation test. A picture is shown to you for several minutes, then taken away. Questions about the picture test your ability to observe both details and larger elements.

5) Following directions

In many positions in the public service, the employee must be able to carry out written instructions dependably and accurately. You may be given a chart with several columns, each column listing a variety of information. The questions require you to carry out directions involving the information given in the chart.

6) Skills and aptitudes

Performance tests effectively measure some manual skills and aptitudes. When the skill is one in which you are trained, such as typing or shorthand, you can practice. These tests are often very much like those given in business school or high school courses. For many of the other skills and aptitudes, however, no short-time preparation can be made. Skills and abilities natural to you or that you have developed throughout your lifetime are being tested.

Many of the general questions just described provide all the data needed to answer the questions and ask you to use your reasoning ability to find the answers. Your best preparation for these tests, as well as for tests of facts and ideas, is to be at your physical and mental best. You, no doubt, have your own methods of getting into an exam-taking mood and keeping "in shape." The next section lists some ideas on this subject.

IV. KINDS OF QUESTIONS

Only rarely is the "essay" question, which you answer in narrative form, used in civil service tests. Civil service tests are usually of the short-answer type. Full instructions for answering these questions will be given to you at the examination. But in case this is your first experience with short-answer questions and separate answer sheets, here is what you need to know:

1) Multiple-choice Questions

Most popular of the short-answer questions is the "multiple choice" or "best answer" question. It can be used, for example, to test for factual knowledge, ability to solve problems or judgment in meeting situations found at work.

A multiple-choice question is normally one of three types—
- It can begin with an incomplete statement followed by several possible endings. You are to find the one ending which *best* completes the statement, although some of the others may not be entirely wrong.
- It can also be a complete statement in the form of a question which is answered by choosing one of the statements listed.

- It can be in the form of a problem – again you select the best answer.

Here is an example of a multiple-choice question with a discussion which should give you some clues as to the method for choosing the right answer:

When an employee has a complaint about his assignment, the action which will *best* help him overcome his difficulty is to
- A. discuss his difficulty with his coworkers
- B. take the problem to the head of the organization
- C. take the problem to the person who gave him the assignment
- D. say nothing to anyone about his complaint

In answering this question, you should study each of the choices to find which is best. Consider choice "A" – Certainly an employee may discuss his complaint with fellow employees, but no change or improvement can result, and the complaint remains unresolved. Choice "B" is a poor choice since the head of the organization probably does not know what assignment you have been given, and taking your problem to him is known as "going over the head" of the supervisor. The supervisor, or person who made the assignment, is the person who can clarify it or correct any injustice. Choice "C" is, therefore, correct. To say nothing, as in choice "D," is unwise. Supervisors have and interest in knowing the problems employees are facing, and the employee is seeking a solution to his problem.

2) True/False Questions

The "true/false" or "right/wrong" form of question is sometimes used. Here a complete statement is given. Your job is to decide whether the statement is right or wrong.

SAMPLE: A roaming cell-phone call to a nearby city costs less than a non-roaming call to a distant city.

This statement is wrong, or false, since roaming calls are more expensive.

This is not a complete list of all possible question forms, although most of the others are variations of these common types. You will always get complete directions for answering questions. Be sure you understand *how* to mark your answers – ask questions until you do.

V. RECORDING YOUR ANSWERS

Computer terminals are used more and more today for many different kinds of exams.

For an examination with very few applicants, you may be told to record your answers in the test booklet itself. Separate answer sheets are much more common. If this separate answer sheet is to be scored by machine – and this is often the case – it is highly important that you mark your answers correctly in order to get credit.

An electronic scoring machine is often used in civil service offices because of the speed with which papers can be scored. Machine-scored answer sheets must be marked with a pencil, which will be given to you. This pencil has a high graphite content which responds to the electronic scoring machine. As a matter of fact, stray dots may register as answers, so do not let your pencil rest on the answer sheet while you are pondering the correct answer. Also, if your pencil lead breaks or is otherwise defective, ask for another.

Since the answer sheet will be dropped in a slot in the scoring machine, be careful not to bend the corners or get the paper crumpled.

The answer sheet normally has five vertical columns of numbers, with 30 numbers to a column. These numbers correspond to the question numbers in your test booklet. After each number, going across the page are four or five pairs of dotted lines. These short dotted lines have small letters or numbers above them. The first two pairs may also have a "T" or "F" above the letters. This indicates that the first two pairs only are to be used if the questions are of the true-false type. If the questions are multiple choice, disregard the "T" and "F" and pay attention only to the small letters or numbers.

Answer your questions in the manner of the sample that follows:

32. The largest city in the United States is
    A. Washington, D.C.
    B. New York City
    C. Chicago
    D. Detroit
    E. San Francisco

1) Choose the answer you think is best. (New York City is the largest, so "B" is correct.)
2) Find the row of dotted lines numbered the same as the question you are answering. (Find row number 32)
3) Find the pair of dotted lines corresponding to the answer. (Find the pair of lines under the mark "B.")
4) Make a solid black mark between the dotted lines.

VI. BEFORE THE TEST

Common sense will help you find procedures to follow to get ready for an examination. Too many of us, however, overlook these sensible measures. Indeed, nervousness and fatigue have been found to be the most serious reasons why applicants fail to do their best on civil service tests. Here is a list of reminders:

- Begin your preparation early – Don't wait until the last minute to go scurrying around for books and materials or to find out what the position is all about.
- Prepare continuously – An hour a night for a week is better than an all-night cram session. This has been definitely established. What is more, a night a week for a month will return better dividends than crowding your study into a shorter period of time.
- Locate the place of the exam – You have been sent a notice telling you when and where to report for the examination. If the location is in a different town or otherwise unfamiliar to you, it would be well to inquire the best route and learn something about the building.
- Relax the night before the test – Allow your mind to rest. Do not study at all that night. Plan some mild recreation or diversion; then go to bed early and get a good night's sleep.
- Get up early enough to make a leisurely trip to the place for the test – This way unforeseen events, traffic snarls, unfamiliar buildings, etc. will not upset you.
- Dress comfortably – A written test is not a fashion show. You will be known by number and not by name, so wear something comfortable.

- Leave excess paraphernalia at home – Shopping bags and odd bundles will get in your way. You need bring only the items mentioned in the official notice you received; usually everything you need is provided. Do not bring reference books to the exam. They will only confuse those last minutes and be taken away from you when in the test room.
- Arrive somewhat ahead of time – If because of transportation schedules you must get there very early, bring a newspaper or magazine to take your mind off yourself while waiting.
- Locate the examination room – When you have found the proper room, you will be directed to the seat or part of the room where you will sit. Sometimes you are given a sheet of instructions to read while you are waiting. Do not fill out any forms until you are told to do so; just read them and be prepared.
- Relax and prepare to listen to the instructions
- If you have any physical problem that may keep you from doing your best, be sure to tell the test administrator. If you are sick or in poor health, you really cannot do your best on the exam. You can come back and take the test some other time.

VII. AT THE TEST

The day of the test is here and you have the test booklet in your hand. The temptation to get going is very strong. Caution! There is more to success than knowing the right answers. You must know how to identify your papers and understand variations in the type of short-answer question used in this particular examination. Follow these suggestions for maximum results from your efforts:

1) Cooperate with the monitor

The test administrator has a duty to create a situation in which you can be as much at ease as possible. He will give instructions, tell you when to begin, check to see that you are marking your answer sheet correctly, and so on. He is not there to guard you, although he will see that your competitors do not take unfair advantage. He wants to help you do your best.

2) Listen to all instructions

Don't jump the gun! Wait until you understand all directions. In most civil service tests you get more time than you need to answer the questions. So don't be in a hurry. Read each word of instructions until you clearly understand the meaning. Study the examples, listen to all announcements and follow directions. Ask questions if you do not understand what to do.

3) Identify your papers

Civil service exams are usually identified by number only. You will be assigned a number; you must not put your name on your test papers. Be sure to copy your number correctly. Since more than one exam may be given, copy your exact examination title.

4) Plan your time

Unless you are told that a test is a "speed" or "rate of work" test, speed itself is usually not important. Time enough to answer all the questions will be provided, but this does not mean that you have all day. An overall time limit has been set. Divide the total time (in minutes) by the number of questions to determine the approximate time you have for each question.

5) Do not linger over difficult questions

If you come across a difficult question, mark it with a paper clip (useful to have along) and come back to it when you have been through the booklet. One caution if you do this – be sure to skip a number on your answer sheet as well. Check often to be sure that you have not lost your place and that you are marking in the row numbered the same as the question you are answering.

6) Read the questions

Be sure you know what the question asks! Many capable people are unsuccessful because they failed to *read* the questions correctly.

7) Answer all questions

Unless you have been instructed that a penalty will be deducted for incorrect answers, it is better to guess than to omit a question.

8) Speed tests

It is often better NOT to guess on speed tests. It has been found that on timed tests people are tempted to spend the last few seconds before time is called in marking answers at random – without even reading them – in the hope of picking up a few extra points. To discourage this practice, the instructions may warn you that your score will be "corrected" for guessing. That is, a penalty will be applied. The incorrect answers will be deducted from the correct ones, or some other penalty formula will be used.

9) Review your answers

If you finish before time is called, go back to the questions you guessed or omitted to give them further thought. Review other answers if you have time.

10) Return your test materials

If you are ready to leave before others have finished or time is called, take ALL your materials to the monitor and leave quietly. Never take any test material with you. The monitor can discover whose papers are not complete, and taking a test booklet may be grounds for disqualification.

VIII. EXAMINATION TECHNIQUES

1) Read the general instructions carefully. These are usually printed on the first page of the exam booklet. As a rule, these instructions refer to the timing of the examination; the fact that you should not start work until the signal and must stop work at a signal, etc. If there are any *special* instructions, such as a choice of questions to be answered, make sure that you note this instruction carefully.

2) When you are ready to start work on the examination, that is as soon as the signal has been given, read the instructions to each question booklet, underline any key words or phrases, such as *least, best, outline, describe* and the like. In this way you will tend to answer as requested rather than discover on reviewing your paper that you *listed without describing*, that you selected the *worst* choice rather than the *best* choice, etc.

3) If the examination is of the objective or multiple-choice type – that is, each question will also give a series of possible answers: A, B, C or D, and you are called upon to select the best answer and write the letter next to that answer on your answer paper – it is advisable to start answering each question in turn. There may be anywhere from 50 to 100 such questions in the three or four hours allotted and you can see how much time would be taken if you read through all the questions before beginning to answer any. Furthermore, if you come across a question or group of questions which you know would be difficult to answer, it would undoubtedly affect your handling of all the other questions.

4) If the examination is of the essay type and contains but a few questions, it is a moot point as to whether you should read all the questions before starting to answer any one. Of course, if you are given a choice – say five out of seven and the like – then it is essential to read all the questions so you can eliminate the two that are most difficult. If, however, you are asked to answer all the questions, there may be danger in trying to answer the easiest one first because you may find that you will spend too much time on it. The best technique is to answer the first question, then proceed to the second, etc.

5) Time your answers. Before the exam begins, write down the time it started, then add the time allowed for the examination and write down the time it must be completed, then divide the time available somewhat as follows:
   - If 3-1/2 hours are allowed, that would be 210 minutes. If you have 80 objective-type questions, that would be an average of 2-1/2 minutes per question. Allow yourself no more than 2 minutes per question, or a total of 160 minutes, which will permit about 50 minutes to review.
   - If for the time allotment of 210 minutes there are 7 essay questions to answer, that would average about 30 minutes a question. Give yourself only 25 minutes per question so that you have about 35 minutes to review.

6) The most important instruction is to *read each question* and make sure you know what is wanted. The second most important instruction is to *time yourself properly* so that you answer every question. The third most important instruction is to *answer every question*. Guess if you have to but include something for each question. Remember that you will receive no credit for a blank and will probably receive some credit if you write something in answer to an essay question. If you guess a letter – say "B" for a multiple-choice question – you may have guessed right. If you leave a blank as an answer to a multiple-choice question, the examiners may respect your feelings but it will not add a point to your score. Some exams may penalize you for wrong answers, so in such cases *only*, you may not want to guess unless you have some basis for your answer.

7) Suggestions
   a. Objective-type questions
      1. Examine the question booklet for proper sequence of pages and questions
      2. Read all instructions carefully
      3. Skip any question which seems too difficult; return to it after all other questions have been answered
      4. Apportion your time properly; do not spend too much time on any single question or group of questions

5. Note and underline key words – *all, most, fewest, least, best, worst, same, opposite*, etc.
6. Pay particular attention to negatives
7. Note unusual option, e.g., unduly long, short, complex, different or similar in content to the body of the question
8. Observe the use of "hedging" words – *probably, may, most likely*, etc.
9. Make sure that your answer is put next to the same number as the question
10. Do not second-guess unless you have good reason to believe the second answer is definitely more correct
11. Cross out original answer if you decide another answer is more accurate; do not erase until you are ready to hand your paper in
12. Answer all questions; guess unless instructed otherwise
13. Leave time for review

   b. Essay questions
     1. Read each question carefully
     2. Determine exactly what is wanted. Underline key words or phrases.
     3. Decide on outline or paragraph answer
     4. Include many different points and elements unless asked to develop any one or two points or elements
     5. Show impartiality by giving pros and cons unless directed to select one side only
     6. Make and write down any assumptions you find necessary to answer the questions
     7. Watch your English, grammar, punctuation and choice of words
     8. Time your answers; don't crowd material

8) Answering the essay question

Most essay questions can be answered by framing the specific response around several key words or ideas. Here are a few such key words or ideas:

M's: manpower, materials, methods, money, management
P's: purpose, program, policy, plan, procedure, practice, problems, pitfalls, personnel, public relations

   a. Six basic steps in handling problems:
     1. Preliminary plan and background development
     2. Collect information, data and facts
     3. Analyze and interpret information, data and facts
     4. Analyze and develop solutions as well as make recommendations
     5. Prepare report and sell recommendations
     6. Install recommendations and follow up effectiveness

   b. Pitfalls to avoid
     1. *Taking things for granted* – A statement of the situation does not necessarily imply that each of the elements is necessarily true; for example, a complaint may be invalid and biased so that all that can be taken for granted is that a complaint has been registered

2. *Considering only one side of a situation* – Wherever possible, indicate several alternatives and then point out the reasons you selected the best one
3. *Failing to indicate follow up* – Whenever your answer indicates action on your part, make certain that you will take proper follow-up action to see how successful your recommendations, procedures or actions turn out to be
4. *Taking too long in answering any single question* – Remember to time your answers properly

IX. AFTER THE TEST

Scoring procedures differ in detail among civil service jurisdictions although the general principles are the same. Whether the papers are hand-scored or graded by machine we have described, they are nearly always graded by number. That is, the person who marks the paper knows only the number – never the name – of the applicant. Not until all the papers have been graded will they be matched with names. If other tests, such as training and experience or oral interview ratings have been given, scores will be combined. Different parts of the examination usually have different weights. For example, the written test might count 60 percent of the final grade, and a rating of training and experience 40 percent. In many jurisdictions, veterans will have a certain number of points added to their grades.

After the final grade has been determined, the names are placed in grade order and an eligible list is established. There are various methods for resolving ties between those who get the same final grade – probably the most common is to place first the name of the person whose application was received first. Job offers are made from the eligible list in the order the names appear on it. You will be notified of your grade and your rank as soon as all these computations have been made. This will be done as rapidly as possible.

People who are found to meet the requirements in the announcement are called "eligibles." Their names are put on a list of eligible candidates. An eligible's chances of getting a job depend on how high he stands on this list and how fast agencies are filling jobs from the list.

When a job is to be filled from a list of eligibles, the agency asks for the names of people on the list of eligibles for that job. When the civil service commission receives this request, it sends to the agency the names of the three people highest on this list. Or, if the job to be filled has specialized requirements, the office sends the agency the names of the top three persons who meet these requirements from the general list.

The appointing officer makes a choice from among the three people whose names were sent to him. If the selected person accepts the appointment, the names of the others are put back on the list to be considered for future openings.

That is the rule in hiring from all kinds of eligible lists, whether they are for typist, carpenter, chemist, or something else. For every vacancy, the appointing officer has his choice of any one of the top three eligibles on the list. This explains why the person whose name is on top of the list sometimes does not get an appointment when some of the persons lower on the list do. If the appointing officer chooses the second or third eligible, the No. 1 eligible does not get a job at once, but stays on the list until he is appointed or the list is terminated.

X. HOW TO PASS THE INTERVIEW TEST

The examination for which you applied requires an oral interview test. You have already taken the written test and you are now being called for the interview test – the final part of the formal examination.

You may think that it is not possible to prepare for an interview test and that there are no procedures to follow during an interview. Our purpose is to point out some things you can do in advance that will help you and some good rules to follow and pitfalls to avoid while you are being interviewed.

What is an interview supposed to test?

The written examination is designed to test the technical knowledge and competence of the candidate; the oral is designed to evaluate intangible qualities, not readily measured otherwise, and to establish a list showing the relative fitness of each candidate – as measured against his competitors – for the position sought. Scoring is not on the basis of "right" and "wrong," but on a sliding scale of values ranging from "not passable" to "outstanding." As a matter of fact, it is possible to achieve a relatively low score without a single "incorrect" answer because of evident weakness in the qualities being measured.

Occasionally, an examination may consist entirely of an oral test – either an individual or a group oral. In such cases, information is sought concerning the technical knowledges and abilities of the candidate, since there has been no written examination for this purpose. More commonly, however, an oral test is used to supplement a written examination.

Who conducts interviews?

The composition of oral boards varies among different jurisdictions. In nearly all, a representative of the personnel department serves as chairman. One of the members of the board may be a representative of the department in which the candidate would work. In some cases, "outside experts" are used, and, frequently, a businessman or some other representative of the general public is asked to serve. Labor and management or other special groups may be represented. The aim is to secure the services of experts in the appropriate field.

However the board is composed, it is a good idea (and not at all improper or unethical) to ascertain in advance of the interview who the members are and what groups they represent. When you are introduced to them, you will have some idea of their backgrounds and interests, and at least you will not stutter and stammer over their names.

What should be done before the interview?

While knowledge about the board members is useful and takes some of the surprise element out of the interview, there is other preparation which is more substantive. It *is* possible to prepare for an oral interview – in several ways:

1) Keep a copy of your application and review it carefully before the interview

This may be the only document before the oral board, and the starting point of the interview. Know what education and experience you have listed there, and the sequence and dates of all of it. Sometimes the board will ask you to review the highlights of your experience for them; you should not have to hem and haw doing it.

2) Study the class specification and the examination announcement

Usually, the oral board has one or both of these to guide them. The qualities, characteristics or knowledges required by the position sought are stated in these documents. They offer valuable clues as to the nature of the oral interview. For example, if the job involves supervisory responsibilities, the announcement will usually indicate that knowledge of modern supervisory methods and the qualifications of the candidate as a supervisor will be tested. If so, you can expect such questions, frequently in the form of a hypothetical situation which you are expected to solve. NEVER go into an oral without knowledge of the duties and responsibilities of the job you seek.

3) Think through each qualification required

Try to visualize the kind of questions you would ask if you were a board member. How well could you answer them? Try especially to appraise your own knowledge and background in each area, *measured against the job sought*, and identify any areas in which you are weak. Be critical and realistic – do not flatter yourself.

4) Do some general reading in areas in which you feel you may be weak

For example, if the job involves supervision and your past experience has NOT, some general reading in supervisory methods and practices, particularly in the field of human relations, might be useful. Do NOT study agency procedures or detailed manuals. The oral board will be testing your understanding and capacity, not your memory.

5) Get a good night's sleep and watch your general health and mental attitude

You will want a clear head at the interview. Take care of a cold or any other minor ailment, and of course, no hangovers.

What should be done on the day of the interview?

Now comes the day of the interview itself. Give yourself plenty of time to get there. Plan to arrive somewhat ahead of the scheduled time, particularly if your appointment is in the fore part of the day. If a previous candidate fails to appear, the board might be ready for you a bit early. By early afternoon an oral board is almost invariably behind schedule if there are many candidates, and you may have to wait. Take along a book or magazine to read, or your application to review, but leave any extraneous material in the waiting room when you go in for your interview. In any event, relax and compose yourself.

The matter of dress is important. The board is forming impressions about you – from your experience, your manners, your attitude, and your appearance. Give your personal appearance careful attention. Dress your best, but not your flashiest. Choose conservative, appropriate clothing, and be sure it is immaculate. This is a business interview, and your appearance should indicate that you regard it as such. Besides, being well groomed and properly dressed will help boost your confidence.

Sooner or later, someone will call your name and escort you into the interview room. *This is it.* From here on you are on your own. It is too late for any more preparation. But remember, you asked for this opportunity to prove your fitness, and you are here because your request was granted.

What happens when you go in?

The usual sequence of events will be as follows: The clerk (who is often the board stenographer) will introduce you to the chairman of the oral board, who will introduce you to the other members of the board. Acknowledge the introductions before you sit down. Do not be surprised if you find a microphone facing you or a stenotypist sitting by. Oral interviews are usually recorded in the event of an appeal or other review.

Usually the chairman of the board will open the interview by reviewing the highlights of your education and work experience from your application – primarily for the benefit of the other members of the board, as well as to get the material into the record. Do not interrupt or comment unless there is an error or significant misinterpretation; if that is the case, do not hesitate. But do not quibble about insignificant matters. Also, he will usually ask you some question about your education, experience or your present job – partly to get you to start talking and to establish the interviewing "rapport." He may start the actual questioning, or turn it over to one of the other members. Frequently, each member undertakes the questioning on a particular area, one in which he is perhaps most competent, so you can expect each member to participate in the examination. Because time is limited, you may also expect some rather abrupt switches in the direction the questioning takes, so do not be upset by it. Normally, a board member will not pursue a single line of questioning unless he discovers a particular strength or weakness.

After each member has participated, the chairman will usually ask whether any member has any further questions, then will ask you if you have anything you wish to add. Unless you are expecting this question, it may floor you. Worse, it may start you off on an extended, extemporaneous speech. The board is not usually seeking more information. The question is principally to offer you a last opportunity to present further qualifications or to indicate that you have nothing to add. So, if you feel that a significant qualification or characteristic has been overlooked, it is proper to point it out in a sentence or so. Do not compliment the board on the thoroughness of their examination – they have been sketchy, and you know it. If you wish, merely say, "No thank you, I have nothing further to add." This is a point where you can "talk yourself out" of a good impression or fail to present an important bit of information. Remember, *you close the interview yourself*.

The chairman will then say, "That is all, Mr. _____, thank you." Do not be startled; the interview is over, and quicker than you think. Thank him, gather your belongings and take your leave. Save your sigh of relief for the other side of the door.

How to put your best foot forward

Throughout this entire process, you may feel that the board individually and collectively is trying to pierce your defenses, seek out your hidden weaknesses and embarrass and confuse you. Actually, this is not true. They are obliged to make an appraisal of your qualifications for the job you are seeking, and they want to see you in your best light. Remember, they must interview all candidates and a non-cooperative candidate may become a failure in spite of their best efforts to bring out his qualifications. Here are 15 suggestions that will help you:

1) Be natural – Keep your attitude confident, not cocky

If you are not confident that you can do the job, do not expect the board to be. Do not apologize for your weaknesses, try to bring out your strong points. The board is interested in a positive, not negative, presentation. Cockiness will antagonize any board member and make him wonder if you are covering up a weakness by a false show of strength.

2) Get comfortable, but don't lounge or sprawl

Sit erectly but not stiffly. A careless posture may lead the board to conclude that you are careless in other things, or at least that you are not impressed by the importance of the occasion. Either conclusion is natural, even if incorrect. Do not fuss with your clothing, a pencil or an ashtray. Your hands may occasionally be useful to emphasize a point; do not let them become a point of distraction.

3) Do not wisecrack or make small talk

This is a serious situation, and your attitude should show that you consider it as such. Further, the time of the board is limited – they do not want to waste it, and neither should you.

4) Do not exaggerate your experience or abilities

In the first place, from information in the application or other interviews and sources, the board may know more about you than you think. Secondly, you probably will not get away with it. An experienced board is rather adept at spotting such a situation, so do not take the chance.

5) If you know a board member, do not make a point of it, yet do not hide it

Certainly you are not fooling him, and probably not the other members of the board. Do not try to take advantage of your acquaintanceship – it will probably do you little good.

6) Do not dominate the interview

Let the board do that. They will give you the clues – do not assume that you have to do all the talking. Realize that the board has a number of questions to ask you, and do not try to take up all the interview time by showing off your extensive knowledge of the answer to the first one.

7) Be attentive

You only have 20 minutes or so, and you should keep your attention at its sharpest throughout. When a member is addressing a problem or question to you, give him your undivided attention. Address your reply principally to him, but do not exclude the other board members.

8) Do not interrupt

A board member may be stating a problem for you to analyze. He will ask you a question when the time comes. Let him state the problem, and wait for the question.

9) Make sure you understand the question

Do not try to answer until you are sure what the question is. If it is not clear, restate it in your own words or ask the board member to clarify it for you. However, do not haggle about minor elements.

10) Reply promptly but not hastily

A common entry on oral board rating sheets is "candidate responded readily," or "candidate hesitated in replies." Respond as promptly and quickly as you can, but do not jump to a hasty, ill-considered answer.

11) Do not be peremptory in your answers

A brief answer is proper – but do not fire your answer back. That is a losing game from your point of view. The board member can probably ask questions much faster than you can answer them.

12) Do not try to create the answer you think the board member wants

He is interested in what kind of mind you have and how it works – not in playing games. Furthermore, he can usually spot this practice and will actually grade you down on it.

13) Do not switch sides in your reply merely to agree with a board member

Frequently, a member will take a contrary position merely to draw you out and to see if you are willing and able to defend your point of view. Do not start a debate, yet do not surrender a good position. If a position is worth taking, it is worth defending.

14) Do not be afraid to admit an error in judgment if you are shown to be wrong

The board knows that you are forced to reply without any opportunity for careful consideration. Your answer may be demonstrably wrong. If so, admit it and get on with the interview.

15) Do not dwell at length on your present job

The opening question may relate to your present assignment. Answer the question but do not go into an extended discussion. You are being examined for a *new* job, not your present one. As a matter of fact, try to phrase ALL your answers in terms of the job for which you are being examined.

Basis of Rating

Probably you will forget most of these "do's" and "don'ts" when you walk into the oral interview room. Even remembering them all will not ensure you a passing grade. Perhaps you did not have the qualifications in the first place. But remembering them will help you to put your best foot forward, without treading on the toes of the board members.

Rumor and popular opinion to the contrary notwithstanding, an oral board wants you to make the best appearance possible. They know you are under pressure – but they also want to see how you respond to it as a guide to what your reaction would be under the pressures of the job you seek. They will be influenced by the degree of poise you display, the personal traits you show and the manner in which you respond.

ABOUT THIS BOOK

This book contains tests divided into Examination Sections. Go through each test, answering every question in the margin. We have also attached a sample answer sheet at the back of the book that can be removed and used. At the end of each test look at the answer key and check your answers. On the ones you got wrong, look at the right answer choice and learn. Do not fill in the answers first. Do not memorize the questions and answers, but understand the answer and principles involved. On your test, the questions will likely be different from the samples. Questions are changed and new ones added. If you understand these past questions you should have success with any changes that arise. Tests may consist of several types of questions. We have additional books on each subject should more study be advisable or necessary for you. Finally, the more you study, the better prepared you will be. This book is intended to be the last thing you study before you walk into the examination room. Prior study of relevant texts is also recommended. NLC publishes some of these in our Fundamental Series. Knowledge and good sense are important factors in passing your exam. Good luck also helps. So now study this Passbook, absorb the material contained within and take that knowledge into the examination. Then do your best to pass that exam.

EXAMINATION SECTION

EXAMINATION SECTION
TEST 1

DIRECTIONS: Each question or incomplete statement is followed by several suggested answers or completions. Select the one that BEST answers the question or completes the statement. *PRINT THE LETTER OF THE CORRECT ANSWER IN THE SPACE AT THE RIGHT.*

1. Representations of human knowledge used in expert systems generally include each of the following EXCEPT
    A. frames
    B. semantic nets
    C. fuzzy logic
    D. rules

2. Routines performed to verify input data and correct errors prior to processing are known as
    A. edit checks
    B. pilots
    C. control aids
    D. data audits

3. Which of the following statements about database management systems is generally FALSE?
   They
    A. are able to separate logical and physical views of data
    B. eliminate data confusion by providing central control of data creation and definitions
    C. reduce data redundancy
    D. involve slight increases in program development and maintenance costs

4. In systems theory, there is a *what-if* method of treating uncertainty that explores the effect on the alternatives of environmental change. This method is generally referred to as _____ analysis.
    A. sensitivity
    B. contingency
    C. a fortiori
    D. systems

5. One of the core capabilities of a decision support system (DSS) is the logical and mathematical manipulation of data_____ a capability referred to as
    A. control aids
    B. representations
    C. memory aids
    D. operations

6. What is the term for the ability to move software from one generation of hardware to another more powerful generation?
    A. Adaptability
    B. Interoperability
    C. Multitasking
    D. Migration

7. In an enterprise information system, which of the following is considered to be an input control?
    A. Documentation of operating procedures
    B. Reviews of processing logs
    C. Verification of control totals
    D. Program testing

8. Low-speed transmission of data that occurs one character at a time is described as

   A. asynchronous
   B. unchained
   C. phased
   D. unstructured

9. Which of the following is a disadvantage associated with the use of relational databases?

   A. Limited ability to combine information from different sources
   B. Simplicity in maintenance
   C. Relatively slower speed of operation
   D. Limited flexibility regarding ad hoc queries

10. When all the elements in a system are in the same category, _____ is said to be at a minimum.

    A. uncertainty
    B. synergy
    C. inefficiency
    D. entropy

11. Which of the following is most likely to rely on parallel processing?

    A. Minicomputer
    B. Workstation
    C. Microcomputer
    D. Supercomputer

12. In imaging systems, what is the term for the device that allows a user to identify and retrieve a specific document?

    A. Forward chain
    B. Index server
    C. Knowledge base
    D. Search engine

13. Which of the following systems exists at the strategic level of an organization?

    A. Decision support system (DSS)
    B. Executive support system (ESS)
    C. Knowledge work system (KWS)
    D. Management information system (MIS)

14. What is the term for the secondary storage device on which a complete operating system is stored?

    A. Central Processing Unit
    B. Microprocessor
    C. Optical code recognizer
    D. System residence drive

15. Which of the following is NOT a type of knowledge work system (KWS)?

    A. Investment workstations
    B. Virtual reality systems
    C. Computer-aided design (CAD)
    D. Decision support system (DSS)

16. A transmission over a telecommunications network in which data can flow two ways, but in only one direction at a time, is described as

    A. simplex
    B. half duplex
    C. full duplex
    D. multiplex

17. The functions of knowledge workers in an organization generally include each of the following EXCEPT

    A. updating knowledge
    B. managing documentation of knowledge
    C. serving as internal consultants
    D. acting as change agents

18. The predominant programming language for business was

    A. Perl   B. COBOL   C. FORTRAN   D. SGML

19. In general, the technology associated with reduced instruction set (RISC) computers is most appropriate for

    A. decision support systems (DSS)
    B. network communications
    C. scientific and workstation computing
    D. desktop publishing

20. Which of the following signifies the international reference model for linking different types of computers and networks?

    A. WAN   B. ISDN   C. TCP/IP   D. OSI

21. The main difference between neural networks and expert systems is that neural networks

    A. seek a generalized capability to learn
    B. program solutions
    C. are aimed at solving one specific problem at a time
    D. seek to emulate or model a person's way of solving a set of problems

22. Which of the following is not a management benefit associated with end-user development of information systems?

    A. Reduced application backlog
    B. Increased user satisfaction
    C. Simplified testing and documentation procedures
    D. Improved requirements determination

23. Which of the following is NOT an example of an output control associated with information systems?

    A. Balancing output totals with input and processing totals
    B. formal procedures and documentation specifying recipients of reports and checks
    C. Error handling
    D. Review of computer processing logs

24. Of the following statements about the evolutionary planning method of strategic information systems design, which is FALSE?
It is

    A. a top-down method
    B. high adaptive
    C. best for use in a dynamic environment
    D. susceptible to domination by a few users

25. In a relational database, a row or record is referred to as a(n)

    A. applet
    B. key field
    C. tuple
    D. bitmap

KEY (CORRECT ANSWERS)

1.	C	11.	D
2.	A	12.	B
3.	D	13.	B
4.	B	14.	D
5.	D	15.	D
6.	D	16.	B
7.	C	17.	B
8.	A	18.	B
9.	C	19.	C
10.	A	20.	D

21. A
22. C
23. C
24. A
25. C

TEST 2

DIRECTIONS: Each question or incomplete statement is followed by several suggested answers or completions. Select the one that BEST answers the question or completes the statement. *PRINT THE LETTER OF THE CORRECT ANSWER IN THE SPACE AT THE RIGHT.*

1. The technical staff of an organization are most likely to be users of a(n)   1.____

    A. transaction processing system (TPS)
    B. management information system (MIS)
    C. decision support system (DSS)
    D. knowledge work system (KWS)

2. The predefined packet of data in some LANs, which includes data indicating the sender, receiver, and whether the packet is in use, is known as a   2.____

    A. bus   B. check   C. token   D. parity

3. Which of the following is NOT a typical characteristic of hypertext and hypermedia applications?   3.____

    A. Users given commands to delete frames
    B. Independence from GUI environment
    C. Frames displayed in windows
    D. In shared systems, concurrent access to hypermedia data

4. Which of the following is a commercial digital information service that exists to provide business information?   4.____

    A. Prodigy   B. Dialog   C. Quotron   D. Lexis

5. Which of the following is NOT a characteristic of an enterprise MIS?   5.____

    A. Standardization
    B. Requires systems managers
    C. Homogeneous data
    D. Supports multiple applications

6. In workgroup information systems, the simplest type of group conferencing is referred to as a(n)   6.____

    A. videoconference   B. group meeting
    C. asynchronous meeting   D. electronic bulletin board

7. Which of the following is an advantage associated with the LAN model of multi-user systems?   7.____

    A. Reliability of many computers
    B. Unlimited performance
    C. Centralized control
    D. Relative independence from technology

8. The main advantage of digital private branch exchanges over other local networking options is that they   8.____

5

A. make use of existing phone lines
B. have a greater geographical range
C. perform important traffic control functions
D. can generally transmit larger volumes of data

9. In a typical organization, tactical and operational planning of an MIS would be the responsibility of the

   A. steering committee and MIS managers
   B. project teams
   C. operations personnel and end users
   D. chief information officer

10. _____ code is the term for program instructions written in a high-level language before translation into machine language.

    A. Spaghetti   B. Source   C. Macro   D. Pseudo

11. In its current form, the technology of electronic data interchange (EDI) is appropriate for transmitting all of the following EXCEPT

    A. purchase orders   B. bills of lading
    C. solicitations   D. invoices

12. Which of the following types of applications is generally most dependent on the graphical user interface (GUI) environment?

    A. Electronic communication
    B. Desktop publishing
    C. Word processing
    D. Spreadsheet

13. Which of the following is a logical design element of an information system?

    A. Hardware specifications   B. Output media
    C. Data models   D. Software

14. A processing system rejects an order transaction for 10,000 units, on the basis that no order larger than 70 units had been placed previously. This is an example of a

    A. check digit   B. format check
    C. reasonableness check   D. dependency check

15. The concentric circle on the surface area of a disk, on which data are stored as magnetized spots, is known as a

    A. cylinder   B. track   C. register   D. sector

16. Which of the following storage media generally has the slowest access speed?

    A. Optical disk   B. RAM
    C. Magnetic disk   D. Cache

17. The most time-consuming element of system conversion plans is

    A. hardware upgrading   B. personnel training
    C. documentation   D. data conversion

18. In most organizations, the chief information officer is given a rank equivalent to

   A. project manager
   B. data administrator
   C. team leader
   D. vice president

19. Which of the following statements about the prototyping approach to systems development is FALSE?
    It is

   A. especially valuable for designing an end-user interface
   B. generally better suited for larger applications
   C. most useful when there is some uncertainty about requirements or design solutions
   D. as iterative process

20. What is the term for the final step in system reengineering, when the revised specifications are used to generate new, structure program code for a structured and maintainable system?

   A. Direct cutover
   B. Reverse engineering
   C. Workflow engineering
   D. Forward engineering

21. Which of the following are included in an MIS audit?
   I. Physical facilities
   II. Telecommunications
   III. Control systems
   IV. Manual procedures
   The CORRECT answer is:

   A. I, IV
   B. II, III
   C. I, II, III
   D. I, II, III, IV

22. In the traditional systems life cycle model, which of the following stages occurs EARLIEST?

   A. Programming
   B. Design
   C. Installation
   D. Systems study

23. Which of the following concerns is addressed by front-end CASE (Computer-Assisted Software Engineering) tools?

   A. Testing
   B. Analysis
   C. Maintenance
   D. Coding

24. In an individual MIS, the most commonly used analytical application is a

   A. statistical program
   B. gateway
   C. spreadsheet
   D. utility

25. Certain kinds of expert systems use the property of inheritance to organize and classify knowledge when the knowledge base is composed of easily identifiable chunks or objects of interrelated characteristics. These systems are known specifically as

   A. political models
   B. rule bases
   C. formal control tools
   D. semantic nets

KEY (CORRECT ANSWERS)

1.	D	11.	C
2.	C	12.	B
3.	B	13.	C
4.	B	14.	C
5.	C	15.	B
6.	D	16.	C
7.	A	17.	D
8.	A	18.	D
9.	A	19.	B
10.	B	20.	D

21. D
22. D
23. B
24. C
25. D

TEST 3

DIRECTIONS: Each question or incomplete statement is followed by several suggested answers or completions. Select the one that BEST answers the question or completes the statement. *PRINT THE LETTER OF THE CORRECT ANSWER IN THE SPACE AT THE RIGHT.*

1. Of an organization's total MIS budget, the majority can be expected to be spent on 1._____

   A. training
   B. programming
   C. operations
   D. administration

2. Each of the following is an element of the installation stage in the traditional model of a systems life cycle EXCEPT 2._____

   A. testing
   B. programming
   C. conversion
   D. training

3. For network applications in which some processing must be centralized and some can be performed locally, which of the following configurations is most appropriate? 3._____

   A. Bus B. Ring C. Star D. Token ring

4. In systems development, the main difference between strategic analysis and enterprise analysis is that 4._____

   A. enterprise analysis makes use of the personal interview
   B. enterprise analysis produces a smaller data set
   C. strategic analysis is used exclusively in profit concerns
   D. strategic analysis tends to have a broader focus

5. Each of the following is a type of source data automation technology EXCEPT 5._____

   A. magnetic ink character recognition (MICR)
   B. touch screen
   C. bar code
   D. optical character recognition (OCR)

6. The main DISADVANTAGE associated with the parallel strategy of information system conversion is that 6._____

   A. run and personnel costs are extremely high
   B. it presents many difficulties in the area of documentation
   C. it provides no fallback in case of trouble
   D. it does not provide a clear picture of how the system will eventually operate throughout the entire organization

7. Which of the following types of systems is most appropriate for solving unstructured problems? 7._____

   A. Expert system
   B. Executive support system (ESS)
   C. Management information system (MIS)
   D. Decision support system (DSS)

8. In terms of information ethics, what is the term for the existence of laws that permit individuals to recover damages done to them by actors, systems, or organizations?

    A. Liability
    B. Subrogation
    C. Accountability
    D. Due process

9. Descriptions that focus on the dynamic aspects of a system's structure, or on change, evolution, and processes in general, are described as

    A. charismatic
    B. synchronic
    C. motile
    D. diachronic

10. One of the features of object-oriented programming is that all objects in a certain group have all the characteristics of that group. This feature is defined as

    A. base
    B. legitimacy
    C. class
    D. multiplexing

11. The most prominent data manipulation language in use today is

    A. Intellect
    B. Easytrieve
    C. APL
    D. SQL

12. Feasibility studies involved in systems analysis tend to focus on three specific areas. _____ feasibility is NOT one of these.

    A. Technical
    B. Operational
    C. Cultural
    D. Economic

13. A computer may sometimes handle programs more efficiently by dividing them into small fixed-or variable-length portions, with only a small portion stored in primary memory at one time. This is known as

    A. multitasking
    B. caching
    C. allocation
    D. virtual storage

14. Of the following applications, end-user computing is MOST appropriate for the development of

    A. scheduling systems for optimal production
    B. tracking daily trades of securities
    C. systems for handling air traffic
    D. systems for the development of three-dimensional graphics

15. In a hierarchical database, what is the term for the specialized data element attached to a record that shows the absolute or relative address of another record?

    A. Tickler   B. Index   C. Register   D. Pointer

16. For which of the following types of databases is the direct file access method most appropriate?

    A. Bank statements
    B. Payroll
    C. On-line hotel reservations
    D. Government benefits program

17. A _____ structured project with _____ technology requirements would most likely involve the lowest degree of risk to an organization.

    A. small, highly; low
    B. small, flexibly; high
    C. large, flexibly; high
    D. large, highly; low

18. Historically, under federal law creators of intellectual property were protected against copying by others for a period of

    A. 10 years
    B. 17 years
    C. 28 years
    D. the creator's natural life

19. Most modern secondary storage devices operate at speeds measured in

    A. nanoseconds
    B. milliseconds
    C. microseconds
    D. seconds

20. Which of the following signifies the international standard for transmitting voice, video, and data to support a wide range of service over the public telephone lines?

    A. HTML
    B. ISDN
    C. TCP/IP
    D. ASCII

21. An important limitation associated with executive support systems today is that they

    A. use data from different systems designed for very different purposes
    B. have a narrow range of easy-to-use desktop analytical tools
    C. are used almost exclusively by executives
    D. do an inadequate job of filtering data

22. Each of the following is an element of the systems study stage in the traditional model of a systems life cycle EXCEPT

    A. identifying objectives to be attained by a solution
    B. determining whether the organization has a problem that can be solved with a system
    C. analyzing problems with existing systems
    D. describing alternative solutions

23. The commercial software product *Lotus Notes* is an example of

    A. intelligent agent software
    B. groupware
    C. a star network
    D. electronic data interchange (EDI)

24. Weaknesses in a system's _____ controls may create errors or failures in new or modified systems.

    A. data file security
    B. implementation
    C. physical hardware
    D. software

25. Which of the following is a term used to describe the ability to move from summary data to more specific levels of detail? 25.___

    A. Drill down
    B. Forward chaining
    C. Downsizing
    D. Semantic networking

KEY (CORRECT ANSWERS)

1. C
2. B
3. C
4. D
5. B

6. A
7. B
8. A
9. D
10. C

11. D
12. C
13. D
14. D
15. D

16. C
17. A
18. C
19. B
20. B

21. A
22. B
23. B
24. B
25. A

EXAMINATION SECTION
TEST 1

DIRECTIONS: Each question or incomplete statement is followed by several suggested answers or completions. Select the one that BEST answers the question or completes the statement. *PRINT THE LETTER OF THE CORRECT ANSWER IN THE SPACE AT THE RIGHT.*

1. Which is NOT an example of a system?

    A. Management
    B. Organization
    C. Document
    D. Computer
    E. Education

2. The systems process has three components.
   Which is NOT one of the components?

    A. Programming
    B. Development
    C. Design
    D. Analysis
    E. None of the above

3. Which of the following lists the three components of the systems process in the CORRECT order?

    A. Development, analysis, and design
    B. Analysis, design, and development
    C. Design, analysis, and development
    D. Development, design, and analysis
    E. Analysis, development, and design

4. Which component of the systems process comes FIRST?

    A. Design
    B. Development
    C. Review
    D. Analysis
    E. Audit

5. Which component of the systems process comes THIRD?

    A. Design
    B. Development
    C. Review
    D. Analysis
    E. Audit

6. Which component of the systems process comes SECOND?

    A. Design
    B. Development
    C. Review
    D. Analysis
    E. Audit

7. Which component of the systems process comes FIFTH?

    A. Design
    B. Development
    C. Review
    D. Analysis
    E. Audit

8. Who USUALLY initiates the systems process?

    A. An outside vendor
    B. A user
    C. Management
    D. Computer services staff
    E. The Federal government

9. During which phase of the systems process are programs written? 9.____

   A. Analysis B. Design C. Development
   D. Review E. None of the above

10. During which phase of the systems process are alternatives identified? 10.____

    A. Design
    B. Analysis
    C. Development
    D. Review
    E. None of the above

11. During which phase of the systems process are files defined? 11.____

    A. Design B. Analysis
    C. Development D. Programming
    E. During all phases

12. Which of the following is NOT a part of computer-based systems? 12.____

    A. Hardware B. Software C. People
    D. Procedures E. None of the above

13. Which of the following is an example of data? 13.____
    The

    A. cost of a pair of running shoes
    B. average price of a pair of running shoes
    C. most popular style of running shoe
    D. average size shoe worn by men
    E. average size shoe worn by women

14. Which of the following is an example of information? 14.____

    A. The cost of a pair of running shoes
    B. The number of pairs of size 8D shoes on hand
    C. The average price of a pair of running shoes
    D. All of the above
    E. None of the above

15. The adjusting of a system is called 15.____

    A. hardware B. feedback C. procedures
    D. alternatives E. programming

16. Which of the following is NOT a common accounting system? 16.____

    A. Payroll B. Spreadsheet C. Inventory
    D. Payables E. Receivables

17. Studying the way an organization retrieves and processes data is systems 17.____

    A. development B. design C. feedback
    D. analysis E. hardware

18. Deciding on the formats of reports, storage methods, and data collection methods is systems   18.____

    A. design B. analysis C. development
    D. feedback E. procedures

19. Implementing, programming, testing, and training is systems   19.____

    A. design B. development C. analysis
    D. procedures E. alternatives

20. An organization that converts raw materials into finished or semi-finished goods is classified as   20.____

    A. not-for-profit B. service
    C. governmental D. manufacturing
    E. none of the above

21. An organization that performs tasks for consumers is classified as   21.____

    A. service B. not-for-profit
    C. governmental D. manufacturing
    E. none of the above

22. Line structure has overall responsibility and authority assigned to the   22.____

    A. bottom level workers B. top level managers
    C. middle level workers D. bottom level managers
    E. union representatives

23. An example of a department typically serving in a staff relationship is   23.____

    A. sales B. manufacturing C. finance
    D. personnel E. marketing

24. Depicts the lines of authority between individuals and departments in a business   24.____

    A. flowchart B. data flow diagram
    C. Warnier Orr chart D. organization chart
    E. Gantt chart

25. The person responsible for performing the systems study is the   25.____

    A. systems analyst
    B. user
    C. manager of computing services
    D. vice-president of business services
    E. director of information services

KEY (CORRECT ANSWERS)

1. C
2. A
3. B
4. D
5. B

6. A
7. E
8. B
9. C
10. B

11. A
12. E
13. A
14. C
15. B

16. B
17. D
18. A
19. B
20. D

21. A
22. B
23. D
24. D
25. A

TEST 2

DIRECTIONS: Each question or incomplete statement is followed by several suggested answers or completions. Select the one that BEST answers the question or completes the statement. *PRINT THE LETTER OF THE CORRECT ANSWER IN THE SPACE AT THE RIGHT.*

1. The MOST important aspect of an analyst's relationship with a user is   1.____

    A. friendship B. respect C. comraderie
    D. knowledge E. rapport

2. The device used MOST often to enter data into the computer is the   2.____

    A. keypunch B. card reader C. terminal
    D. printer E. disk drive

3. The MOST rapidly growing segment of the computer marketplace is   3.____

    A. personal computers B. terminals
    C. mainframes D. mini-computers
    E. keypunch machines

4. The set of rules, guidelines, and tools that facilitate effective system analysis, design, and development is known as   4.____

    A. Warnier Orr methodology
    B. structured methodology
    C. Gantt chart
    D. PERT charts
    E. critical path methodology

5. Which is a DISADVANTAGE of the structured methodology?   5.____

    A. Lower maintenance costs
    B. Lower long-term costs
    C. Improved system reliability
    D. Higher design costs
    E. More flexible systems

6. Which is NOT an advantage of the structured methodology?   6.____

    A. Lower long-term costs
    B. Lower maintenance costs
    C. Wider user involvement
    D. Improved system reliability
    E. None of the above

7. Which is NOT an advantage of the structured methodology?   7.____

    A. More easily enhanced systems
    B. Fewer system failures
    C. Reduced likelihood of errors
    D. More understandable programs
    E. None of the above

8. This person was NOT a developer of the structured programming methodology.

   A. Bohm B. Hollerith C. Jacopini
   D. Dijkstra E. Stevens

9. A(n) _____ is used in a data flow diagram to depict a process.

   A. square B. line C. circle
   D. rectangle E. arrow

10. A(n) _____ is used to show a flow of data in a data flow diagram.

    A. square B. parallelogram C. trapezoid
    D. arrow E. circle

11. The report resulting from detailed analysis is called the

    A. feasibility study B. implementation study
    C. analysis study D. systems study
    E. narrative analysis

12. The report resulting from the design stage is called the

    A. feasibility study B. system specifications
    C. system audit D. implementation plan
    E. system study

13. The final review of a completed system is called the

    A. feasibility study B. system specifications
    C. systems study D. system audit
    E. implementation plan

14. Ordering of any new hardware for a system would take place during

    A. analysis B. design C. development
    D. training E. conversion

15. Developing operational procedures of the computer center staff would take place during

    A. analysis B. design C. development
    D. training E. conversion

16. Defining the data requirements would take place during

    A. analysis B. design C. development
    D. training E. conversion

17. Writing program specifications would take place during

    A. analysis B. design C. development
    D. training E. conversion

18. Drawing a model of the new systems data flow would take place during

    A. analysis B. design C. development
    D. training E. conversion

19. Listing costs and benefits of a new system would take place during 19.____

    A. analysis B. design C. development
    D. training E. conversion

20. MOST business applications programs are written in 20.____

    A. FORTRAN B. BASIC C. COBOL D. PASCAL E. ADA

KEY (CORRECT ANSWERS)

1. E	11. A
2. C	12. B
3. A	13. D
4. B	14. B
5. D	15. C
6. E	16. B
7. E	17. B
8. B	18. B
9. C	19. A
10. D	20. C

EXAMINATION SECTION
TEST 1

DIRECTIONS: Each question or incomplete statement is followed by several suggested answers or completions. Select the one that BEST answers the question or completes the statement. *PRINT THE LETTER OF THE CORRECT ANSWER IN THE SPACE AT THE RIGHT.*

1. A square in a data flow diagram symbolizes

    A. a file
    B. a terminal
    C. a printer
    D. destination of data
    E. conversion of input data to output data

    1._____

2. A three-sided rectangle in a data flow diagram symbolizes

    A. a file
    B. a terminal
    C. a printer
    D. destination of data
    E. conversion of input data to output data

    2._____

3. A circle in a data flow diagram symbolizes

    A. a file
    B. a terminal
    C. a printer
    D. destination of data
    E. conversion of input data to output data

    3._____

4. An arrow in a data flow diagram symbolizes

    A. a file
    B. a terminal
    C. the direction of data flow between processes
    D. destination of data
    E. conversion of input data to output data

    4._____

5. Inputs to analysis include

    A. user needs
    B. budget
    C. schedule
    D. amount of time to complete the system
    E. all of the above

    5._____

6. Outputs from analysis include

    A. budget
    B. schedule
    C. documentation
    D. feasibility study
    E. all of the above

    6._____

7. Inputs to analysis do NOT include

   A. management funding
   B. user objectives
   C. expected costs
   D. computer services staff expertise
   E. none of the above

8. The feasibility study is output from which phase of the systems process?

   A. Development   B. Analysis   C. Design
   D. Programming   E. Database design

9. Decomposition or levelling refers to

   A. the feasibility study
   B. analysis documentation
   C. the systems study
   D. expansion of data flow diagrams to more detail levels
   E. expansion of hardware and software to solve user needs

10. The system's cycle begins with a request from

    A. a governmental body
    B. a user
    C. a trade union
    D. the custodian
    E. all of the above could initiate a system's cycle

11. Which of the following is NOT a part of preliminary analysis?

    A. Evaluation of a user request
    B. Drawing the logical system
    C. Analysis of a user request
    D. Management action
    E. All of the above are a part of preliminary analysis

12. When evaluating a user request, the analyst should NOT collect

    A. the user's name
    B. the description of the problem
    C. the problems solution
    D. the date of the request
    E. additional comments as necessary

13. In evaluating a user request, the goal is to isolate the

    A. problem   B. solution
    C. people involved   D. time to be expended
    E. cost savings

14. In evaluating the user request, the analyst will want to

    A. review the organizations sales   B. review the organizations profits
    C. review the organizations costs   D. interview the user
    E. all of the above

15. The period of time in an interview where the analyst establishes rapport is called   15.____

    A. closure   B. questioning   C. warm-up
    D. fact-finding   E. recording

16. The period of time in an interview where the analyst terminates discussion is called   16.____

    A. closure   B. questioning   C. warm-up
    D. fact-finding   E. recording

17. The period of time in an interview where the analyst states the problem and solicits   17.____
    responses is called

    A. closure   B. questioning   C. warm-up
    D. program review   E. initialization

18. Which of the following is NOT a part of the preliminary report?   18.____

    A. Findings
    B. Recommendations
    C. Solution to the problem
    D. Costs and schedules
    E. All of the above are a part of the preliminary report

19. An analyst must   19.____

    A. adapt to evolving technology
    B. remember that systems support people
    C. analyze an organization's needs
    D. determine the firm's requirements
    E. all of the above

20. In conducting a meeting, the analyst should   20.____

    A. prepare an agenda
    B. schedule a conference room
    C. set a time and date for the meeting
    D. invite appropriate personnel
    E. all of the above

KEY (CORRECT ANSWERS)

1.	C	11.	B
2.	A	12.	C
3.	E	13.	A
4.	C	14.	D
5.	A	15.	C
6.	E	16.	A
7.	C	17.	B
8.	B	18.	D
9.	D	19.	E
10.	E	20.	E

TEST 2

DIRECTIONS: Each question or incomplete statement is followed by several suggested answers or completions. Select the one that BEST answers the question or completes the statement. *PRINT THE LETTER OF THE CORRECT ANSWER IN THE SPACE AT THE RIGHT.*

1. In conducting a meeting, the analyst should   1.____

    A. set time limits
    B. circulate an agenda before the meeting
    C. avoid unnecessary meetings
    D. see that the issues are stated
    E. all of the above

2. When evaluating a user request, the analyst should consider   2.____

    A. the corporate logo
    B. the effect of the meeting on fellow analysts
    C. the organization's goals and objectives
    D. the expertise of the user
    E. all of the above

3. Analysis can be levelled into   3.____

    A. preliminary and future analysis
    B. preliminary and detailed analysis
    C. detailed and future analysis
    D. needs assessment
    E. hardware requirements

4. Who approves the preliminary report?   4.____

    A. Management   B. The user   C. The analyst
    D. The government   E. The union

5. Who approves funding for preliminary and detailed analysis?   5.____

    A. The user
    B. The manager of the computer services department
    C. Management
    D. The analyst
    E. None of the above

6. Analysis documentation details   6.____

    A. questions the analyst must ask
    B. background information pertinent to the system
    C. answers to interview questions
    D. solutions that are unworkable
    E. all of the above

7. The feasibility study details

   A. questions the analyst must ask
   B. background information pertinent to the system
   C. answers to interview questions
   D. system objectives
   E. all of the above

8. Systems developed during the 1950's were

   A. statistically or scientifically oriented
   B. mini-computer oriented
   C. micro-computer oriented
   D. user oriented
   E. all of the above

9. Systems developed during the 1980's must be

   A. network oriented
   B. user oriented
   C. user friendly
   D. micro-computer oriented
   E. all of the above

10. Once a decision to continue onto detailed analysis is made by management, all parties concerned should be notified by

    A. memorandum
    B. telephone
    C. word of mouth
    D. rumor
    E. a Christmas letter

11. After an interview, the analyst sends a follow-up memorandum. Which of the following should the memorandum NOT include?

    A. Information gained
    B. Date and time of the interview
    C. Value judgments made by the analyst
    D. Names and titles of personnel interviewed
    E. None of the above

12. Follow-up memoranda help establish

    A. accuracy
    B. rapport
    C. personal relationships
    D. documentation
    E. all of the above

13. A preliminary report to management includes

    A. problem review and software solutions
    B. problem review and recommendations
    C. recommendations and software solutions
    D. software and hardware solution
    E. personnel change recommendations

14. A preliminary report should include

    A. transcripts of interviews
    B. all working papers collected during analysis
    C. lists of telephone calls made
    D. list of alternatives
    E. all of the above

15. After reviewing the preliminary report, management may decide to

    A. continue to detailed analysis
    B. terminate the study
    C. delay any further study for a short time
    D. choose an alternative other than the one recommended by the analyst
    E. all of the above

16. The preliminary report should be

    A. delivered verbally to management
    B. filled with computer jargon
    C. written and distributed in advance
    D. given to users for a decision
    E. given to computer services staff for decision

17. In MOST cases, management will

    A. terminate the systems process at their first opportunity
    B. choose an alternative not recommended by the analyst
    C. delay a decision for six to eight months
    D. decide to continue to detailed analysis
    E. none of the above

18. During the interview, the analyst should

    A. be a listener
    B. do all the talking
    C. make value judgments
    D. ask personal questions
    E. have a pre-determined solution in mind

19. In selecting the appropriate people to interview, the analyst should consult a(n)

    A. data flow diagram
    B. entity diagram
    C. organization chart
    D. organized specification chart
    E. any of the above

20. Before doing anything, the analyst should

    A. review old programs pertinent to the request
    B. review the user's request
    C. examine the user work area
    D. test the system software for proper operation
    E. talk with other analysts about the user

KEY (CORRECT ANSWERS)

1.	E	11.	C
2.	C	12.	E
3.	B	13.	B
4.	A	14.	D
5.	C	15.	E
6.	B	16.	C
7.	D	17.	D
8.	A	18.	A
9.	E	19.	C
10.	A	20.	B

EXAMINATION SECTION
TEST 1

DIRECTIONS: Each question or incomplete statement is followed by several suggested answers or completions. Select the one that BEST answers the question or completes the statement. *PRINT THE LETTER OF THE CORRECT ANSWER IN THE SPACE AT THE RIGHT.*

1. The analysis phase of the systems process is divided into

    A. preliminary and detailed
    B. input and output
    C. hardware and software
    D. costs and benefits
    E. people and procedures

2. Detailed analysis involves

    A. an investigation of the existing system
    B. how an organization collects data
    C. how an organization processes data
    D. how to improve the processing of data
    E. all of the above

3. When conducting the detailed analysis, the analyst consults with

    A. users
    B. outside vendors
    C. management
    D. other members of the computing services staff
    E. all of the above

4. Before starting the detailed analysis, the analyst reviews the

    A. organization chart
    B. preliminary report
    C. database design
    D. screen lay-out formats
    E. program specifications

5. An output from analysis is the

    A. program specifications
    B. module specifications
    C. input data collection screen designs
    D. feasibility study
    E. database design

6. The FIRST task in detailed analysis is

    A. fact-finding
    B. presentation of analysis to management
    C. review and assignment
    D. interviewing users
    E. none of the above

7. The LAST task in detailed analysis is

   A. fact-finding
   B. presentation of analysis to management
   C. review and assignment
   D. interviewing users
   E. none of the above

8. A tool an analyst can use to assist in scheduling is the

   A. data flow diagram   B. Gantt chart
   C. Warnier-Orr diagram   D. CPM chart
   E. HIPO chart

9. In a Gantt chart, events are listed

   A. as bars
   B. as rectangles
   C. along the left-hand side
   D. along the right-hand side
   E. across the bottom

10. In a Gantt chart personnel assigned to events are listed

    A. as bars
    B. as rectangles
    C. along the left-hand side
    D. along the right-hand side
    E. across the bottom

11. As tasks are completed, the analyst updates the Gantt chart by

    A. filling in hollow horizontal bars
    B. completing a worksheet
    C. reviewing the task assignments
    D. notifying management
    E. none of the above

12. Fact-finding means an analyst needs to

    A. learn as much as possible about the system
    B. interview all company personnel
    C. review the systems study
    D. review the program specifications
    E. talk with hardware vendors

13. Which one of the following is NOT a part of the four W's the analyst must ask?

    A. Who is involved?
    B. What do you do?
    C. While you do it, what are others doing?
    D. Why do you do it the way you do?
    E. When do you do it?

14. Users should be notified of the detailed analysis by 14.____

    A. telephone call
    B. general meeting
    C. a memorandum
    D. a notice in the company newsletter
    E. a meeting at the water fountain

15. During fact-finding, the analyst gathers together 15.____

    A. forms
    B. documents
    C. interviews with key staff members
    D. observations of the system
    E. all of the above

16. Questions posed on a questionnaire should be 16.____

    A. worded using computer jargon
    B. lead the responder to draw conclusions
    C. nonthreatening
    D. vague
    E. general purpose

17. Which type of questionnaire gives respondents a specific set of potential answers? 17.____

    A. Open-ended   B. Multiple choice
    C. Rating   D. Rank
    E. None of the above

18. Which type of questionnaire gives respondents a chance to answer in their own words? 18.____

    A. Open-ended   B. Multiple choice
    C. Rating   D. Rank
    E. None of the above

19. Which type of questionnaire gives respondents a chance to show their satisfaction? 19.____

    A. Open-ended   B. Multiple choice
    C. Rating   D. Rank
    E. None of the above

20. Which type of questionnaire gives respondents a chance to prioritize on a high to low basis? 20.____

    A. Open-ended   B. Multiple choice
    C. Rating   D. Rank
    E. None of the above

KEY (CORRECT ANSWERS)

1.	A	11.	A
2.	E	12.	A
3.	E	13.	C
4.	B	14.	C
5.	D	15.	E
6.	C	16.	C
7.	B	17.	B
8.	B	18.	A
9.	C	19.	C
10.	E	20.	D

TEST 2

DIRECTIONS: Each question or incomplete statement is followed by several suggested answers or completions. Select the one that BEST answers the question or completes the statement. *PRINT THE LETTER OF THE CORRECT ANSWER IN THE SPACE AT THE RIGHT.*

1. When observing an existing system, an analyst should be   1.____

    A. an observer
    B. a questioner
    C. a part of the system
    D. an answerer
    E. making value judgments

2. When observing a system, it is LIKELY that the system will   2.____

    A. not function
    B. operate 500% faster
    C. operate 50% slower
    D. operate differently than it normally does
    E. none of the above

3. After observing the system, the analyst can draw a diagram of the logical system using which of the following techniques?   3.____

    A. Data flow diagram
    B. Gantt chart
    C. HIPO chart
    D. PERT chart
    E. IPD chart

4. A data flow diagram that shows a system in its MOST general form is called a(n) _____ DFD.   4.____

    A. analysis
    B. context
    C. levelled
    D. decomposed
    E. system

5. A data flow diagram that shows a system in its MOST specific form is called a(n) _____ DFD.   5.____

    A. analysis
    B. context
    C. levelled
    D. decomposed
    E. system

6. To draw a DFD, the analyst should   6.____

    A. identify activities
    B. isolate data flows
    C. look for duplication of data flows
    D. show the relationship between activities
    E. all of the above

7. An alternative that should ALWAYS be considered is   7.____

    A. computerize the process
    B. program the process
    C. do nothing
    D. contract the process to outsiders
    E. all of the above

33

2 (#2)

8. In deciding what to do, the analyst should consider

   A. costs
   B. benefits
   C. alternatives
   D. personnel
   E. all of the above

9. In deciding what to do, the analyst should consider

   A. buying a packaged solution
   B. buying a main-frame computer
   C. hiring additional staff
   D. contracting the solution to an outside organization
   E. none of the above

10. The final report of findings produced during analysis is called

    A. the systems study
    B. the feasibility study
    C. the program study
    D. the programming specifications
    E. none of the above

11. The final report of findings is reviewed by

    A. management
    B. users
    C. computer services staff
    D. the analyst
    E. all of the above

12. The final report of findings is approved by

    A. management
    B. users
    C. computer services staff
    D. the analyst
    E. all of the above

13. If a recommendation is made to buy software from an outside supplier, the analyst should ask the supplier about

    A. cost and performance
    B. security and compatability
    C. upgrading and updates
    D. training and support
    E. all of the above

14. Future costs for a system should be

    A. added together
    B. ignored
    C. discounted
    D. subtracted from current costs
    E. all of the above

15. Besides costs, the analyst needs to calculate

    A. future needs
    B. benefits
    C. the impact on competitors

D. the impact on users
E. alternative messages

16. Which of the following costs MUST be considered in any alternative? 16.____

    A. System design
    B. System development
    C. Hardware
    D. Software and training
    E. All of the above

17. When collecting documents for an accounts payable system, which is NOT appropriate? 17.____

    A. Invoice
    B. Packing slip
    C. Monthly statement
    D. Check
    E. All are appropriate

18. Who should sign the analysis authorization memorandum? 18.____

    A. The analyst
    B. A manager
    C. A user
    D. A programmer
    E. Any of the above

19. An output from analysis is the 19.____

    A. program specifications
    B. module specifications
    C. input data collection screen designs
    D. analysis documentation
    E. database design

20. During interviews, an analyst functions like a(n) 20.____

    A. newspaper reporter
    B. architect
    C. programmer
    D. supervisor
    E. friend or co-worker

KEY (CORRECT ANSWERS)

1.	A	11.	E
2.	D	12.	A
3.	A	13.	E
4.	B	14.	C
5.	A	15.	B
6.	E	16.	E
7.	C	17.	C
8.	E	18.	B
9.	A	19.	D
10.	B	20.	A

EXAMINATION SECTION
TEST 1

DIRECTIONS: Each question or incomplete statement is followed by several suggested answers or completions. Select the one that BEST answers the question or completes the statement. *PRINT THE LETTER OF THE CORRECT ANSWER IN THE SPACE AT THE RIGHT.*

1. Knowledge work systems are most typically used by each of the following personnel EXCEPT

    A. middle managers
    B. salespeople
    C. engineers
    D. accountants

2. A media-oriented description of a system's operations is BEST represented by a(n)

    A. systems flowchart
    B. system requirements plan
    C. Gantt chart
    D. program flowchart

3. During preliminary analysis, a feasibility group will study the three fundamental operations of an existing system.
   Which of the following is NOT one of these operations?

    A. Output of information
    B. Data processing
    C. Coding
    D. Data preparation and input

4. Normally, the starting point of any systems design is to determine the

    A. output
    B. hardware
    C. throughput
    D. users

5. From its beginnings, the total time required for an entire systems analysis and design process to be completed will MOST likely be

    A. 6-12 months
    B. 12-18 months
    C. 2-3 years
    D. 3-5 years

6. In a data flow diagram, a square like the one shown at the right would be used to represent

    A. input to the system
    B. a terminal
    C. magnetic tape
    D. a display

7. A _____ systems conversion takes place when the old system is switched off and the new one is started up.

    A. day-one   B. direct   C. parallel   D. pilot

8. The MOST common reason for the failure of an information system is

    A. faulty programming
    B. hardware obsolescence
    C. interface complications
    D. faulty problem identification

37

9. A personnel record in a master file consists of the following fields, containing the indicated number of characters.

Field	Number of Characters
Identication number	5
Social Security number	9
Name	25
Address	35
Sex	2
Code number	1

If the master file contains 2,000 transactions, then approximately how many characters would the file be expected to hold?

A. 56,000 B. 115,500 C. 154,000 D. 231,000

10. Which of the following is NOT one of the primary elements of a data flow diagram?

A. Process B. External entity
C. Rule number D. Data store

11. During systems design, each of the following is a consideration involving input EXCEPT

A. media B. validity checking
C. volume D. security

12. The MAIN advantage involved with the use of pilot systems conversion is

A. speed of conversion process
B. provides constant backup media
C. makes file conversion unnecessary
D. minimizes problems by confining operations

13. _____ is NOT a type of systems control.

A. Auditing B. Contingency planning
C. Data security D. Data control

14. In a _____ type of systems conversion, various capabilities are added to the system over a number of years.

A. graduated B. pilot C. phased D. indirect

15. Which of the following is NOT a standard classification for a system in terms of cost-effectiveness?

A. Risky B. Safe
C. Pioneering D. Prudent

16. _____ accounts for the GREATEST expenditure involved in the cost of creating and maintaining a system.

A. Systems design
B. Equipment
C. Evaluation and maintenance
D. Implementation

17. Which of the following is NOT one of the procedures involved in program development? 17._____

    A. Program preparation
    B. Systems audit evaluation
    C. Scheduling
    D. Testing

18. The PRIMARY purpose of the systems analysis phase of the entire analysis and design process is to 18._____

    A. compose an accurate data flow diagram
    B. determine input, output, and processing requirements
    C. determine whether to modify the existing system or convert completely to a new one
    D. consider the people who will be interacting with the new system

19. Which of the following is NOT a major problem associated with systems building? 19._____

    A. Coordination costs
    B. Hardware currency
    C. Requirements analysis
    D. Record keeping

20. Typically, a workable system is the output of the _____ phase of systems analysis and design. 20._____

    A. systems development
    B. systems analysis
    C. systems design
    D. implementation

21. The MOST reliable means of obtaining information about an existing system can be obtained through the use of 21._____

    A. observations
    B. personal interviews
    C. questionnaires
    D. written forms

22. The purpose of a printer spacing chart is to 22._____

    A. represent the exact format of a system's output
    B. assist in data validity checking
    C. coordinate all related fields into a single report
    D. describe the input data needed to produce the system's output

23. The FIRST procedure in a system test plan is usually _____ testing. 23._____

    A. crash proof
    B. system
    C. personnel
    D. unit

24. The cost-benefit analysis of a proposed system is USUALLY performed during the _____ phase of analysis and design. 24._____

    A. systems design
    B. systems analysis
    C. preliminary analysis
    D. implementation

25. The MOST significant output of the systems analysis phase of the entire analysis and design process is the 25._____

    A. detailed system design
    B. system requirements plan
    C. installed and operational system
    D. preliminary plan

KEY (CORRECT ANSWERS)

1. B
2. A
3. C
4. A
5. C

6. A
7. B
8. D
9. C
10. C

11. D
12. D
13. A
14. C
15. A

16. D
17. B
18. C
19. B
20. A

21. B
22. A
23. D
24. A
25. B

TEST 2

DIRECTIONS: Each question or incomplete statement is followed by several suggested answers or completions. Select the one that BEST answers the question or completes the statement. *PRINT THE LETTER OF THE CORRECT ANSWER IN THE SPACE AT THE RIGHT.*

1. Systems maintenance involves three important factors that are considered during the design and development phases of a project. Which of the following is NOT one of these three?

    A. Structured programming
    B. System documentation
    C. System auditing
    D. Anticipation of future needs

2. In a data flow diagram, an open-ended rectangle like the one shown at the right would be used to represent

    A. an invoice
    B. a punched card
    C. data storage
    D. data preparation

3. Systems design reports normally include each of the following EXCEPT a(n)

    A. review of the problems associated with the present system
    B. overview of the proposed system
    C. summation of the major findings of the cost-benefit analysis
    D. list of hardware recommended for the proposed system

4. A _____ group is NOT usually involved in a typical systems project team.

    A. vendor
    B. user
    C. management
    D. programming

5. The _____ method of systems conversion is typically the riskiest.

    A. parallel   B. pilot   C. day-one   D. direct

6. The PRIMARY purpose of a decision table used in systems analysis is to

    A. describe the sequence of operations that must be performed to obtain a computer solution to a problem
    B. represent all the combinations of conditions that must be satisfied before an action can be taken
    C. describe the operations to be performed by the system, with a major emphasis on the media involved, as well as the workstations through which they pass
    D. graphically depict the flow of data and the processes that change or transform data throughout the system

7. Which of the following is used to describe a system's necessary input data?

    A. Systems flowchart
    B. CRT layout form
    C. Data flow diagram
    D. Record layout form

41

8. The LONGEST phase involved in the systems analysis and design process is the _____ phase.

   A. implementation
   B. systems design
   C. systems development
   D. preliminary analysis

9. The systems development phase of analysis and design normally includes each of the following EXCEPT

   A. purchase of equipment
   B. program testing
   C. user training
   D. program development

10. In cases where it is too expensive to convert a system's old files and applications, a(n) _____ system conversion is commonly used.

    A. parallel   B. pilot   C. direct   D. day-one

11. The PRIMARY purpose of an audit trail is to

    A. trace specific input data to its related output
    B. error-check a new systems program
    C. locate workstations where unauthorized users are at work
    D. check data validity

12. A system requirements plan typically includes each of the following EXCEPT

    A. description of how existing system works
    B. hardware requirements for the new system
    C. information necessary for the new system
    D. major problems of existing system

13. A _____ is typically a member of the programming group of a systems project team.

    A. vendor
    B. user
    C. management
    D. librarian

14. The implementation phase of systems analysis and design does NOT usually include

    A. training
    B. auditing
    C. programming
    D. system conversion

15. The _____ is a document created by the systems project team that takes into account the organizational constraints and the personnel involved in using a new system.

    A. system requirements report
    B. statement of objectives
    C. test plan
    D. request for proposal

16. Which of the following is used as an aid to scheduling system operations?

    A. Gantt chart
    B. Circle graph
    C. Chief programmer
    D. Head node

17. The MAIN disadvantage associated with parallel systems conversion is that

    A. it usually takes more time than all other approaches
    B. there is costly duplication of personnel efforts and equipment
    C. confusion is involved in constant switch-overs
    D. no backup is provided

18. Transaction processing systems are LEAST likely to be used by

    A. knowledge professionals
    B. data entry specialists
    C. customers
    D. clerks

19. When a new system is used in its entirety only in one locality or area, _____ is being practiced.

    A. batch processing   B. live data analysis
    C. pilot conversion   D. file conversion

20. Which of the following is NOT a software tool that has been developed to help a systems analyst build better systems in a more timely and cost-effective manner?

    A. CAD tools   B. Project management tools
    C. Prototyping   D. CASE tools

21. Action stubs and conditions entries are components of the

    A. program flowchart   B. decision table
    C. system flowchart   D. Gantt chart

22. When both an old and a new system are run simultaneously for a period of time to ensure the new system's proper operation, _____ is being practiced.

    A. incremental auditing   B. file conversion
    C. parallel conversion   D. direct switch-over

23. The FIRST operation performed during the implementation phase of analysis and design is usually

    A. file conversion   B. systems evaluation
    C. systems conversion   D. auditing

24. Typically, programming accounts for _____% of the hours spent on systems analysis and design.

    A. 10   B. 20   C. 35   D. 45

25. In a data flow diagram, a circle like the one shown at the right would be used to represent

    A. output from the system
    B. a single file
    C. a manual action
    D. a process that transforms data in some way

KEY (CORRECT ANSWERS)

1. C
2. C
3. D
4. A
5. D

6. B
7. D
8. C
9. C
10. D

11. A
12. B
13. D
14. C
15. B

16. A
17. B
18. A
19. C
20. A

21. B
22. C
23. A
24. B
25. D

EXAMINATION SECTION
TEST 1

DIRECTIONS: Each question or incomplete statement is followed by several suggested answers or completions. Select the one that *BEST* answers the question or completes the statement. *PRINT THE LETTER OF THE CORRECT ANSWER IN THE SPACE AT THE RIGHT.*

1. A form such as a sales invoice is called a(n) _____ document.   1.____

    A. audit
    B. original
    C. source
    D. input
    E. machine-readable

2. A complete computer system will consist of people, procedures, hardware, software and   2.____

    A. tasks
    B. data
    C. input/output devices
    D. programs
    E. all of the above

3. The person responsible for programming applications such as payroll, inventory, accounts receivable, etc. is the   3.____

    A. systems programmer
    B. lead programmer
    C. applications programmer
    D. computer analyst
    E. computer operator

4. A documented record of transactions through the entire processing cycle is called a(n)   4.____

    A. transaction log
    B. source document
    C. object document
    D. audit trail
    E. control tape

5. Which of the following BEST describes the steps involved in completing a project by a computer systems analyst?   5.____

    A. Problem analysis, problem design, coding, testing, debugging
    B. Flowcharting, coding, testing
    C. System design, testing, maintenance
    D. Preliminary investigation, detailed investigation, system design, system development, system implementation and evaluation, system maintenance
    E. Detailed investigation, reports to management, programming, installation, testing

6. When initially collecting data to conduct a systems project, the computer system analyst should collect data from people via   6.____

    A. multiple choice questionnaires
    B. fill-in the blank questionnaires
    C. open-ended questionnaires
    D. observing their work habits
    E. personal interviews

7. The MOST commonly used tool by analysts today to graphically illustrate the flow of data through a system is by

   A. flowcharts
   B. Warnier-Orr diagrams
   C. Gantt Charts
   D. the Nassi-Schneiderman Chart
   E. data flow diagrams

8. Of input, output, processing, storage methods, and procedures, the one designed first by the analyst is

   A. input
   B. output
   C. processing
   D. storage methods
   E. procedures

9. A list and description of all of the data elements required in a system is listed in a(n)

   A. audit trail
   B. compilation listing
   C. data dictionary
   D. transaction journal
   E. system documentation

10. System controls are instituted to

    A. prevent computer fraud
    B. ensure valid input of data
    C. ensure that reports contain valid information
    D. ensure data is processed completely and accurately
    E. all of the above

11. A method used by the analyst to document the scheduling of the completion of a project is a(n)

    A. flowchart
    B. hierarchy chart
    C. Gantt chart
    D. Warnier-Orr diagram
    E. data flow diagram

12. A method of converting a manual system to an automated system whereby both systems are run simultaneously, whereupon the results are compared and the new system is phased in, is called _____ conversion.

    A. parallel
    B. test-site
    C. direct
    D. concurrent
    E. hybrid

13. The MOST important skill or requirement of the analyst is

    A. good communication skills
    B. proper academic background
    C. good programming skills
    D. good management skills
    E. technical expertise

14. If the analyst fails to consult with the payroll department before developing a new payroll system, the analyst failed to follow the guideline of

    A. developing a structured system
    B. developing a *top-down* system
    C. developing a system with the end-user's needs being of paramount importance
    D. providing for future expansion and change
    E. all of the above

15. In most cases, a request for computer services should originate from

    A. the computer analyst's department
    B. upper level management
    C. the users of the requested system
    D. lower management
    E. mid-management

16. The records contained in the _____ file are *usually* created from source documents. They are later read in to update other, more permanent files

    A. master   B. detail   C. summary
    D. transaction   E. temporary

17. The device which is MOST commonly used for input into the computer system is the

    A. tape drive   B. printer
    C. video terminal   D. optical disk reader
    E. disk drive

18. The process whereby an analyst compares the expenses against the advantages of a computerized system is called

    A. RFP   B. detailed analysis
    C. cost/benefit analysis D. conversion costing
    E. none of the above

19. Most business computer applications are written in which of the following computer languages?

    A. BASIC   B. RPG   C. C
    D. FORTRAN   E. None of the above

20. When gathering facts to study the procedures and transactions of a system, the analyst should consult

    A. management
    B. users
    C. existing documentation
    D. other members of the computer staff
    E. all of the above

21. Which analysis and design tool used by the computer system analyst shows the levels and subdivisions of a computer system?

    A. Data flow diagram   B. System flowchart
    C. Hierarchy chart   D. Pseudocode
    E. Decision table

22. During the design of input, the analyst establishes

    A. format and layout of reports
    B. how to store data
    C. how to collect data
    D. methods of processing input data
    E. which data is needed by users

23. The analyst establishes systems controls. The purpose of these controls is to detect

    A. computer hardware errors
    B. computer software flaws
    C. data entry errors
    D. errors on printed reports
    E. all of the above

24. The MOST commonly used tool that the analyst uses to design printed output reports is the

    A. video display layout
    B. VTOC
    C. data dictionary
    D. printer layout form
    E. flowchart template

25. In respect to the use of microcomputers, the problem of MOST concern to the systems analyst is the

    A. lack of user friendly software
    B. lack of communications ability with mainframe computers
    C. lack of operating systems
    D. lack of standardization
    E. high cost

KEY (CORRECT ANSWERS)

1. C	11. C
2. B	12. A
3. C	13. A
4. D	14. E
5. D	15. C
6. E	16. D
7. E	17. C
8. B	18. C
9. C	19. E
10. E	20. E

21. C
22. C
23. E
24. D
25. D

TEST 2

DIRECTIONS: Each question or incomplete statement is followed by several suggested answers or completions. Select the one that *BEST* answers the question or completes the statement. *PRINT THE LETTER OF THE CORRECT ANSWER IN THE SPACE AT THE RIGHT.*

1. A type of output document that is also used as an input document is called a _____ document. 1.___

   A. source B. turnaround C. master
   D. transaction E. detail

2. The _____ report reveals all data for every single transaction. 2.___

   A. master B. transaction C. summary
   D. detail E. exception

3. A 9 placed on a report design form is used to indicate 3.___

   A. numeric data B. alphabetic data
   C. quantity data D. page numbering
   E. non-numeric data

4. A Z placed on a report design form is used to indicate 4.___

   A. numeric data B. alphabetic data
   C. zero suppression D. a date
   E. non-numeric edited item

5. An X on a report design form is used to indicate 5.___

   A. alphanumeric data B. zero suppression
   C. page numbering D. numeric data
   E. numbers to be printed as currency

6. The totaling of specific rows and/or columns in a report is called 6.___

   A. auditing B. summarizing
   C. crossfooting D. detailing
   E. control totals

7. A temporary data file is called a _____ file. 7.___

   A. transaction B. scratch C. master
   D. detail E. backup

8. Which type of media has been MOST commonly used for backup files? 8.___

   A. Floppy disk B. Disk cartridges
   C. Video cards D. Magnetic tape
   E. Optical disks

9. The media BEST suited for on-line processing is(are) 9.___

   A. magnetic disk B. magnetic tape
   C. video cards D. magnetic drum
   E. all of the above

10. An advantage of a Data Base Management System is

    A. data integrity
    B. reduced data redundancy
    C. consolidation of files
    D. easier access to data
    E. all of the above

11. A type of Data Base Management System where data is *linked* together via a common data field is called a _____ database.

    A. hierarchial
    B. network
    C. Boyce-Codd
    D. relational
    E. flat file

12. The type of input data validation test that checks for an error in the placement of a decimal point is the _____ test.

    A. batch total
    B. crossfooting
    C. slide
    D. control total
    E. transposition

13. The system analyst may solicit hardware and software proposals from vendors. The analyst will do so by preparing this document.

    A. RFQ   B. RFP   C. RJE   D. TOS   E. OCR

14. This computer language was originally endorsed as the *primary* language to be used on projects authorized by the Department of Defense.

    A. Ada
    B. COBOL
    C. FORTRAN
    D. C
    E. BASIC

15. Which tool is used by the analyst to schedule when and how long an activity should take place to complete a project?

    A. PERT chart
    B. VTOC
    C. HIPO chart
    D. Data dictionary
    E. Data flow diagram

16. Program testing is carried out by computer

    A. analysts
    B. programmers
    C. operators
    D. management
    E. users

17. Which group makes the final decision whether or not a system will be implemented?

    A. management
    B. users
    C. system analysts
    D. programmers
    E. operators

18. Which type of accounting system tracks money owed to a company or organization by clients or customers?

    A. Accounts payable
    B. General ledger
    C. Payroll
    D. Inventory
    E. Accounts receivable

19. Which type of accounting system keeps track of descriptions, reorder points, quantities, costs, and vendors of items on hand?

    A. General ledger
    B. Inventory
    C. Payroll
    D. Accounts receivable
    E. Accounts payable

20. A chronological listing of financial transactions is called a

    A. general journal
    B. general ledger
    C. debits and credits
    D. transaction log
    E. audit trail

21. Automating the inventory control system to include reordering inventory might be in violation of which of the following guideline(s)?

    A. Develop systems that are independent of the organization
    B. Integrate systems but avoid complexity
    C. Determine the proper level of automation
    D. Automate routine, repetitive functions
    E. All of the above

22. A virtual system

    A. requires that programs be written so that they conform to memory size limitations
    B. places an entire software application into memory as it is executed
    C. requires that the programmer divide programs into modules or segments
    D. has methods of dividing programs into pages or segments that are loaded into memory as needed
    E. allows multiple programs to be executed at the same time

23. When a systems analyst solicits hardware and/or software from an outside vendor, the analyst should select the hardware and/or software that

    A. exceeds the minimum operating requirements
    B. meets the organization's needs and is competitively priced
    C. meets the organization's budget
    D. can be delivered on time
    E. is from a major manufacturer of the type of product requested

24. Analysts often gather information through the use of questionnaires. A type of questionnaire which uses very explicit questions and requires a short, written response is called a(n) _____ questionnaire.

    A. open ended
    B. multiple choice
    C. direct response
    D. true/false
    E. closed questions

25. During the preliminary investigation, the analyst will gather information

    A. by interviewing top-level management
    B. from all users, using questionnaires
    C. by reviewing all documentation of the existing system
    D. through time and motion studies, observations and interviews
    E. all of the above

KEY (CORRECT ANSWERS)

1.	B	11.	D
2.	D	12.	C
3.	A	13.	B
4.	C	14.	A
5.	A	15.	A
6.	C	16.	B
7.	B	17.	A
8.	D	18.	E
9.	A	19.	B
10.	E	20.	A

21. C
22. D
23. B
24. C
25. A

EXAMINATION SECTION
TEST 1

DIRECTIONS: Each question or incomplete statement is followed by several suggested answers or completions. Select the one that *BEST* answers the question or completes the statement. *PRINT THE LETTER OF THE CORRECT ANSWER IN THE SPACE AT THE RIGHT.*

1. Data Processing is the

   A. input and output of data
   B. transformation of data into information
   C. production of computer generated reports
   D. collection and dissemination of data
   E. none of the above

   1_____

2. The CORRECT hierarchy of data is

   A. field, file, record, database
   B. character, field, record, file, database
   C. record, file, field, database
   D. bit, byte, record, database
   E. character, file, record, field, database

   2_____

3. Which of the following is an update operation?

   A. Adding data
   B. Deleting data
   C. Changing data
   D. All of the above
   E. None of the above

   3_____

4. The _____ are three MAIN components of a computer generated report.

   A. Control breaks, summaries and headings
   B. Detail lines, control breaks and graphs
   C. Headings, detail lines and summary lines
   D. Page breaks, headings and control breaks
   E. Columns, rows and totals

   4_____

5. A computer generated report with control breaks must have

   A. the data organized in random order
   B. the data being produced from at least two files
   C. the data sorted on a control field
   D. page breaks on each control field
   E. at least two control breaks to be meaningful

   5_____

6. The *primary* types of data processing environments in existence today are

   A. batch and real-time
   B. real-time and on-line
   C. transaction and batch
   D. batch and on-line
   E. on-line and real-time

   6_____

7. The FIRST step in solving a problem with a computer is

   A. coding
   B. debugging
   C. problem analysis
   D. system analysis
   E. problem definition with tools such as flowcharts or data flow diagrams

8. In the hierarchy of arithmetic operations, the operation with the HIGHEST priority is

   A. addition
   B. multiplication
   C. exponentiation
   D. parenthesis
   E. division

9. If A = 10, B = 20 and C - 30, what would be the result of the following operation?
   A * B + C * A

   A. 2,300
   B. 500
   C. 400
   D. 3,000
   E. none of these

10. If A = 5, B = 10 and C = 15, what would be the result of the following operation?
    A + C / (C + A)

    A. 1   B. 5.75   C. C, 10.5   D. 20   E. 15

11. A(n) _____ is a formula developed to solve a problem.

    A. computer program
    B. algorithm
    C. flowchart
    D. problem definition
    E. all of the above

12. The two MAIN data types are

    A. numeric and non-numeric
    B. alphabetic and alphanumeric
    C. numeric and alphabetic
    D. arithmetic and logical
    E. alphabetic and special characters

Questions 13 - 19

DIRECTIONS: Use the following flowchart symbols to answer questions 13-19.

13. Which is used for commenting flowcharts? 13._____

14. Which is a process symbol? 14._____

15. Which is a decision box? 15._____

16. Which is a terminal? 16._____

17. Which is an input output symbol? 17._____

18. Which symbol would be BEST suited for the following expression? Is A > B? 18._____

19. Which symbol would be BEST suited for the following expression? Let tax = sale-price * .08? 19._____

20. An advantage of using a flowchart is that 20._____

    A. it is easy to update
    B. it is well suited for long problems
    C. its symbols are very easily memorized
    D. it graphically represents a problem
    E. all of the above are advantages

21. Flowcharting does NOT indicate 21._____

    A. flow lines   B. sequence
    C. line numbers   D. repetition or looping
    E. logical operations

22. A _____ keeps and maintains the content and description of variable names, file, and field names. 22._____

    A. database   B. data dictionary
    C. encyclopedia of data D. data descriptor
    E. computer program

23. The _____ is the part of a program which may be repeated. 23._____

    A. loop   B. data structure
    C. repetition structure D. logic structure
    E. subroutine structure

24. Employee gross-pay is calculated by multiplying hours by rate. A tax rate of 8% is deducted before arriving at net-pay. 24._____
    Which equation would describe the calculation of gross-pay?

    A. Gross-pay = hours * rate * tax-rate
    B. Gross-pay = hours * rate - tax-rate
    C. Gross-pay = (hours * rate) - .08
    D. Gross-pay = 8 - (hours * rate)
    E. None of these

25. If you deposit $1,000 in a savings account at 8% interest for one year, at the end of the year there will be $1,080.
Which equation would determine the amount in the bank? Amount = 1000*

    A. 8   B. .08   C. 108   D. 1.08   E. 8%

25 __

KEY (CORRECT ANSWERS)

1. B
2. B
3. D
4. C
5. C

6. D
7. C
8. D
9. B
10. B

11. B
12. A
13. D
14. A
15. C

16. B
17. E
18. C
19. A
20. D

21. C
22. B
23. A
24. E
25. D

TEST 2

DIRECTIONS: Each question or incomplete statement is followed by several suggested answers or completions. Select the one that BEST answers the question or completes the statement. PRINT THE LETTER OF THE CORRECT ANSWER IN THE SPACE AT THE RIGHT.

1. The three *primary* program logic structures are

   A. looping, branching and sequence
   B. sequence, selection and iteration
   C. arithmetic, logic and sequence
   D. looping, sequence and logic
   E. arithmetic, logic and branching

   1_____

2. Two basic symbols used by hierarchy charts are

   A. flow lines and circles
   B. process blocks (rectangles) End squares
   C. decision boxes and flow lines
   D. parallelograms and flow lines
   E. flow lines and process blocks (rectangles)

   2_____

3. A _____ is a violation of the rules made by the programmer.

   A. logic error
   B. structure error
   C. syntax error
   D. bug
   E. slip

   3_____

4. _____ verifies transaction data at all input, processing, and output points.

   A. Verification
   B. An audit trail
   C. A transaction log
   D. A transaction journal
   E. A ledger

   4_____

5. _____ file organization arranges files in input sequence.

   A. Random
   B. Direct
   C. Sequential
   D. Relative
   E. Indexed

   5_____

6. _____ refers to the process of examining a program design and reviewing the logic of a program with test data.

   A. Debugging
   B. Desk checking
   C. Stepwise refinement
   D. Verification
   E. Logic testing

   6_____

7. This type of file organization allows a single record to be accessed without accessing the entire file. The location of the record to be accessed is relative to the position of the first record in the file. This paragraph refers to _____ access.

   A. direct
   B. random
   C. serial
   D. relative
   E. indexed

   7_____

59

8. A _____ is a variable which will keep track of the number of occurrences of a certain transaction.

   A. counter
   D. tally
   B. accumulator
   E. register
   C. totaler

9. The _____ report will list all or most of the information in a file.

   A. summary
   D. exception
   B. detail
   E. monitor
   C. transaction

10. Data is *originally* recorded in the _____ document.

    A. transaction
    D. source
    B. object
    E. master
    C. original

11. This verification technique confirms that data being input meets certain input criteria. The data being entered may be compared to a list of values.
    This paragraph refers to the

    A. range test
    C. control totals
    E. class test
    B. matching values
    D. required field

12. This verification technique confirms that data falls within certain limit of values.
    This statement refers to the

    A. range test
    C. control totals
    E. class test
    B. matching values
    D. required field

13. The binary (base 2) symbol equivalent to the decimal (base 10) number 31 is

    A. 31   B. 1111   C. 11111   D. 1011   E. none of these

14. The binary (base 2) symbol equivalent to the decimal (base 10) number 13 is

    A. 1011   B. 1010   C. 1101   D. 1100   E. none of these

15. The decimal (base 10) symbol equivalent to the binary (base 2) number 11101 is

    A. 13   B. 24   C. 19   D. 30   E. none of these

16. The hexadecimal (base 16) symbol equivalent to the decimal (base 10) number 2605 is

    A. A2D
    C. 101000101101
    E. none of the above
    B. 3402
    D. B6C

17. The hexadecimal symbol equivalent to the decimal (base 10) number 59 is

    A. 4A   B. A4   C. 3B   D. B3   E. none of these

18. The binary (base 2) symbol equivalent to the hexadecimal value 4D3CE is

A. 01000000111101010000 B. 00110101110010110001
C. 10001101110010001100 D. 01001101001111001110
E. none of the above

19. The hexadecimal (base 16) symbol equivalent to the binary (base 2) number 100010011010 is

   A. 82C B. 74 C. AC1
   D. 89A E. none of these

20. The octal (base 8) symbol equivalent to the binary (base 2) number l0lll10ll00l is

   A. BD9 B. 42 C. 18
   D. 5731 E. none of these

21. Consider the following input data: John, O Reilly, Johnson, O'Reilly.
    If a computer were to arrange these names according to the standard collating sequence, the output would be

    A. Johnson, John, O Reilly, O'Reilly
    B. John, Johnson, O'Reilly, O Reilly
    C. O'Reilly, O Reilly, Johnson, John
    D. John, Johnson, O Reilly, O'Reilly
    E. both a or c

22. In reference to the diagram below, this flowchart sequence describes

    A. conditional flow B. branching C. repetitive flow
    D. logical flow E. sequential flow

23. Which of the following comparisons would result in a true outcome?

    A. 5 = 10 or 6 = 5 and 8 = 2
    B. 10 = 12 and 6=6
    C. 7 = 4 or 9 = 9 and 4 = 4
    D. 5 = 5 and 3 = 2 or 7 = 7
    E. none of the above

24. Which of the following comparisons would result in a true outcome?

    A. 5 > 6 and 8 > 4
    B. 5 > 6 or 4 > 8
    C. 10 = 10 and 8 < 4 or 8 < 3
    D. 67 = 67 and 101 < 345 or 3 = 9
    E. none of the above

25. Which of the following comparisons would result in a true outcome?

    A. 5 = 6 or 7 < 3
    B. (10 < 12 or 14 = 15) and 9=9
    C. (17 > 10 or 5 < 6) and 5 > 7
    D. 88< = 88 and 99 < 98
    E. none of the above

KEY (CORRECT ANSWERS)

1. B
2. E
3. C
4. B
5. C

6. B
7. D
8. A
9. B
10. D

11. B
12. A
13. C
14. C
15. E

16. A
17. C
18. D
19. D
20. D

21. D
22. E
23. C
24. D
25. B

EXAMINATION SECTION
TEST 1

DIRECTIONS: Each question or incomplete statement is followed by several suggested answers or completions. Select the one that BEST answers the question or completes the statement. *PRINT THE LETTER OF THE CORRECT ANSWER IN THE SPACE AT THE RIGHT.*

1. In defining a program, the analyst reviews the   1.____

    A. data flow diagram   B. module definitions
    C. system specifications   D. analysis walkthrough
    E. All of the above

2. During program definition, the analyst determines the   2.____

    A. programming language to be used
    B. programmers that will code the programs
    C. name of each program
    D. purpose of each program
    E. All of the above

3. In reviewing each circle in the data flow diagram, the analyst will find it yields a   3.____

    A. data flow
    B. program
    C. need for a vendor
    D. need for a computer operator
    E. All of the above

4. Each circle in the data flow diagram is identified by a   4.____

    A. square   B. letter   C. number
    D. rectangle   E. file name

5. Circles in the data flow diagram will have data inflows and   5.____

    A. program names   B. data compression
    C. data concentration   D. data outflows
    E. file names

6. Circles in a data flow diagram will have   6.____

    A. data inflows   B. names
    C. numbers   D. data outflows
    E. All of the above

7. Programs are divided into   7.____

    A. models   B. modules   C. sentences
    D. pseudocode   E. divisions

8. A module has a(n)   8.____

    A. single entry point   B. single exit point
    C. single function   D. finite length
    E. All of the above

9. Module length should be restricted to 24

   A. pages
   B. keystrokes
   C. lines
   D. words
   E. sentences

10. Modularizing is

    A. a part of the structured methodology
    B. a programming language sentence
    C. control structure
    D. repetition structure
    E. coupling method

11. Which of the following is NOT a control structure?

    A. Sequence
    B. Function
    C. Decision
    D. Repetition
    E. All are control structures

12. Which control structure permits testing of values and alternative conditions?

    A. Sequence
    B. Decomposition
    C. Decision
    D. Repetition
    E. Solution

13. Which control structure describes a linear series of actions?

    A. Sequence
    B. Decomposition
    C. Decision
    D. Repetition
    E. Solution

14. Which control structure represents a loop?

    A. Sequence
    B. Decomposition
    C. Decision
    D. Repetition
    E. Solution

15. Which control structure is also known as IF-THEN-ELSE?

    A. Decision
    B. Refinement
    C. Sequence
    D. Decomposition
    E. Repetition

16. Which control structure is also known as WHILE-DO?

    A. Decision
    B. Refinement
    C. Sequence
    D. Decomposition
    E. Repetition

17. Which control structure is also known as REPEAT-UNTIL?

    A. Decision
    B. Refinement
    C. Sequence
    D. Decomposition
    E. Repetition

18. Which control structure is also known as CASE?

    A. Decision
    B. Refinement
    C. Sequence
    D. Decomposition
    E. Repetition

19. The breaking down of a system or module into its elementary components is called

    A. decision
    B. refinement
    C. sequence
    D. lowering
    E. none of the above

20. A synonym for refinement is

    A. decision   B. sequence   C. levelling
    D. coupling   E. recomposition

KEY (CORRECT ANSWERS)

1. A   11. B
2. E   12. C
3. B   13. A
4. C   14. D
5. D   15. A

6. E   16. E
7. B   17. E
8. E   18. A
9. C   19. B
10. A   20. C

TEST 2

DIRECTIONS: Each question or incomplete statement is followed by several suggested answers or completions. Select the one that BEST answers the question or completes the statement. *PRINT THE LETTER OF THE CORRECT ANSWER IN THE SPACE AT THE RIGHT.*

1. Which term stands for the inter-relationship among modules?

    A. Coupling B. Cascading C. Cohesion
    D. Levelling E. Refinement

2. What type of coupling do independent modules exhibit?

    A. Tight B. Loose C. Data
    D. Stamp E. Control

3. What type of coupling do dependent modules exhibit?

    A. Tight B. Loose C. Data
    D. Stamp E. Control

4. Which programming instruction violates the single entry/exit function concept of structured methodology?

    A. PERFORM B. READ C. GO TO
    D. WRITE E. STOP

5. Modules should read from

    A. left to bottom B. top down
    C. bottom up D. right to left
    E. None of the above

6. Which of the following is NOT a criteria in module design?

    A. Identification of system dependent functions
    B. Module length
    C. Single entry/exit/purpose
    D. Minimization of reference to data
    E. None of the above

7. Which of the following is NOT a criteria in module design?

    A. Constructing loosely coupled modules
    B. Avoiding content coupled modules
    C. Testing module cohesion
    D. Naming functions according to their purpose
    E. None of the above

8. Which language is the MOST widely used for business applications?

    A. FORTRAN B. BASIC C. COBOL
    D. Ada E. Pascal

9. Which language is now supported as *the* language of the Department of Defense?

    A. FORTRAN B. BASIC C. COBOL
    D. Ada E. Pascal

10. Which language is MOST often used on home or personal computers? 10.____

    A. FORTRAN B. BASIC C. COBOL
    D. Ada E. Pascal

11. Which language is MOST often the one first-year computer science majors learn? 11.____

    A. FORTRAN B. BASIC C. COBOL
    D. Ada E. Pascal

12. Which of the following is NOT a part of system specifications? 12.____

    A. System overview
    B. Data flow diagram
    C. Output or report designs
    D. Database or schema design
    E. None of the above

13. Which of the following is NOT a part of program specifications? 13.____

    A. Module descriptions B. Program definitions
    C. Module pseudocode D. Module names
    E. None of the above

14. The review of the second phase of the systems process is called the 14.____

    A. analysis walkthrough B. system audit
    C. design walkthrough D. development walkthrough
    E. design overview

15. A design review attempts to locate errors in 15.____

    A. screen formats
    B. costs forecast during analysis
    C. benefits predicted during analysis
    D. management decisions made during analysis
    E. All of the above

16. Outputs from the design review include 16.____

    A. management discussions
    B. direction to progress to development
    C. direction to progress to analysis
    D. system overview
    E. All of the above

17. Who authorizes the development phase of the systems process? 17.____

    A. Users B. Programmers C. Analyst
    D. Management E. All of the above

18. Modularizing a program makes it easier to 18.____

    A. compile B. write Ada statements
    C. read D. write assignment statements
    E. All of the above

19. Modularizing makes it easier to

    A. spot potential errors in the COBOL syntax
    B. spot errors in logic
    C. place responsibility for errors
    D. assign staff for testing
    E. All of the above

20. Which of the following is NOT an output from design?

    A. System specifications   B. Module descriptions
    C. Program specifications   D. Database design
    E. COBOL programs

KEY (CORRECT ANSWERS)

1.	A	11.	E
2.	B	12.	E
3.	A	13.	E
4.	C	14.	C
5.	B	15.	A
6.	E	16.	B
7.	E	17.	D
8.	C	18.	C
9.	D	19.	B
10.	B	20.	E

EXAMINATION SECTION
TEST 1

DIRECTIONS: Each question or incomplete statement is followed by several suggested answers or completions. Select the one that BEST answers the question or completes the statement. *PRINT THE LETTER OF THE CORRECT ANSWER IN THE SPACE AT THE RIGHT.*

1. The purpose of the _____ module is to show the overall flow of data through a program.   1.____
    A. file maintenance
    B. read
    C. control
    D. init

2. An index file consists of the _____ fields.   2.____
    A. key and record number
    B. name and masterfile
    C. date and counter
    D. record number and data address

3. Which of the following is/are used to specify detailed computer operations to implement functions?   3.____
    A. Pseudocode
    B. Structure charts
    C. Data flow charts
    D. Modules

4. The purpose of programming an array into an information system is to allow the user to   4.____
    A. practice random file access
    B. sequentially update files
    C. store several values for the same variable in the internal memory of the computer
    D. access any number of variables without having to script

5. What is the MOST commonly used logic structure in systems programming?   5.____
    A. Decision
    B. Sequential
    C. Case
    D. Loop

6. The _____ module enters data into a program.   6.____
    A. init   B. read   C. control   D. write

7. Control-break modules serve to _____ in systems programming.   7.____
    A. interrupt processing in case of a logic error
    B. transfer data from one processing path to another
    C. interrupt processing in case of a data error
    D. give subtotals for a group of similar records

8. The normal order in which modules are presented to the computer and activated are called   8.____
    A. repetitions
    B. selections
    C. sequences
    D. case constructs

9. The EASIEST to program is the

   A. bubble sort
   B. binary search
   C. sequential search
   D. merge of two lists

10. The instruction to increment a variable by one would be written

    A. COUNTER = COUNTER + 1
    B. SUM = COUNTER + 1
    C. COUNTER = SUM + 1
    D. SUM = SUM + VARIABLE

11. A programmer should create a(n) _____ file for storing completed file updates.

    A. transaction
    B. activity
    C. backup
    D. temporary

12. For the purpose of data validation, a new module will need to be processed from the _____ module.

    A. READ
    B. WRAPUP
    C. CALC
    D. WRITE

13. A _____ module is NOT a type of process data module.

    A. control
    B. print
    C. calculation
    D. read

14. In a written computer solution or program flowchart, a marker is used to indicate that there are no more records to be processed.
    This marker is

    A. EXIT
    B. HF
    C. EOF
    D. END

15. The PRIMARY reason negative logic is used in systems programming is to

    A. provide a way of thinking that is more convenient for people
    B. provide a means for checking data validity
    C. increase the number of variables
    D. decrease the number of tests

16. When creating a random-access information system, a programmer sometimes *chains* modules on top of each other. The purpose of this is to

    A. make the program more interactive
    B. place data in intermediate storage of input and output, to speed up processing
    C. enable the user to use larger programs, and leave more room for data in the internal memory
    D. process all the necessary tasks after files have been updated and processed

17. An information system is programmed to put a mailing list into both alphabetical and zip code order.
    What type of logic structure will be used to program the system?

    A. Decision
    B. Case
    C. Sequential
    D. Loop

18. Which of the following is BASIC code used to disassociate a data file from a program?

    A. END
    B. DATA
    C. CLOSE
    D. DIM

19. Which of the following is used to load an array? 19.____

    A. WRITE module   B. Loop
    C. String   D. Primer read

20. Which of the following is NOT a type of decision logic used in the programming structure? 20.____

    A. True   B. False
    C. Conditional   D. Straight-through

21. _____ are tools primarily of the case logic structure. 21.____

    A. Decision tables   B. Codes
    C. READ modules   D. Variables

22. What type of operator, within an expression or equation, uses numerical or string data as operands, and produces logical data as the resultant? 22.____

    A. Relational   B. Network
    C. Logical   D. Hierarchical

23. In a program flowchart, an assignment instruction would be written 23.____

    A. LET   B. VARIABLE=
    C. READ   D. WRITE AS

24. When a programmer wants the value in one array to point to an element in another array, he uses 24.____

    A. a null file   B. a primer read
    C. a nested loop   D. the pointer technique

25. The purpose of _____ is to eliminate rewriting of identical system processes. 25.____

    A. pseudocode   B. sequences
    C. repetitions   D. modules

KEY (CORRECT ANSWERS)

1. C
2. A
3. A
4. C
5. B

6. B
7. D
8. C
9. C
10. A

11. B
12. A
13. A
14. C
15. D

16. C
17. D
18. C
19. B
20. C

21. B
22. A
23. B
24. D
25. D

TEST 2

DIRECTIONS: Each question or incomplete statement is followed by several suggested answers or completions. Select the one that BEST answers the question or completes the statement. *PRINT THE LETTER OF THE CORRECT ANSWER IN THE SPACE AT THE RIGHT.*

1. What is the term for the summation of values within nonsignificant data fields, such as keys and identification number fields? 1.____

    A. Accumulation
    B. Hash total
    C. Null files
    D. Entry key total

2. The PRIMARY purpose of indicators is to 2.____

    A. maintain the processing of a loop structure
    B. change the processing path
    C. assist in nesting loops or decisions
    D. assist in detecting logic errors

3. Which of the following is NOT a means of converting positive logic to negative logic? 3.____

    A. Changing all <= to >
    B. Changing all < to >
    C. Changing all >= to <
    D. Interchanging all of the THEN set of instructions with the corresponding ELSE set of instructions

4. A programmer writes the instruction SUM = SUM + A(R) into a program flowchart, with R = the number of a specific element in an array, and A(R) = the Rth element of the array. The purpose of this instruction is to 4.____

    A. multiply the data items in an array by the number of elements
    B. incrementalize the elements in an array
    C. accumulate the data items in an array
    D. accumulate the elements in an array

5. The term for altering the normal sequential execution of program statements is 5.____

    A. branching   B. trailing   C. interrupting   D. indicating

6. By using the _____ logic structure, a programmer can enable a user to enter the value of a variable from the keyboard, or from a file, to select one of several options in a list. 6.____

    A. loop   B. sequential   C. case   D. decision

7. Which of the following is BASIC code used to define and reserve areas within memory to be used as program tables? 7.____

    A. RETURN   B. IF   C. REM   D. DIM

8. If a programmer overlays sections of a program on top of each other, she will also have to create a(n) _____ to access any of the modules when requested. 8.____

    A. control module
    B. driver program
    C. string editor
    D. nested loop

9. A HOLD instruction will be supplied for _____ modules.

   A. control-break
   B. end
   C. wrapup
   D. init

10. Data is initially recorded, prior to system input, on a form called the

    A. b-tree
    B. primer buffer
    C. source document
    D. init module

11. The _____ module processes instructions only once during a program, and only at the beginning.

    A. init
    B. control
    C. wrapup
    D. read

12. A programmer should place all data needed to update a master file into a(n) _____ file.

    A. temporary
    B. transaction
    C. read
    D. backup

13. Which of the following instructions is used PRIMARILY in a loop logic structure?

    A. REPEAT/UNTIL
    B. END/EXIT
    C. PROCESS
    D. IF/THEN

14. Program processing ends at a point called the

    A. physical end
    B. control-break
    C. logical end
    D. hash point

15. A company maintains a sequential-accessible database. In the record data dictionary, each of the following items would be created as string data EXCEPT

    A. district number
    B. sales amount
    C. sales date
    D. salesperson name

16. In systems programming and design, developing the _____ would occur FIRST.

    A. IPO chart
    B. algorithms
    C. structure chart
    D. flowcharts

17. In a program flowchart, a temporary file is usually represented as

    A. HF
    B. TEMP
    C. F<
    D. TF

18. The instruction to accumulate a variable A would be written

    A. COUNTER = A + 1
    B. SUM = COUNTER + A
    C. COUNTER = SUM + A
    D. SUM = SUM + A

19. In order to distinguish data items or data fields as separate entities, a programmer uses a symbol known as a(n)

    A. hash mark
    B. null character
    C. delimiter
    D. cursor

20. If a program uses the loop logic structure, the programmer must create a(n) _____ to   20.____
    enter data to process before the loop begins.

    A. primer read   B. clear all
    C. INIT module   D. PROCESS module

21. Each array location is known as a(n)   21.____

    A. stack   B. element
    C. string   D. linked list

22. Which of the following is BASIC code used to link a data file to a program?   22.____

    A. LINK   B. OPEN   C. LET   D. GOTO

23. IF/THEN/ELSE instructions are used in programs that use the _____ logic structure.   23.____

    A. case   B. loop   C. decision   D. array

24. A(n) _____ is used in program problem-solving to stand for a memory location at which   24.____
    a data value is retained.

    A. array   B. variable   C. cell   D. element

25. Which of the following is NOT a type of indicator used in systems programming?   25.____

    A. Trip value   B. Switch
    C. Nested loop   D. Flag

KEY (CORRECT ANSWERS)

1.	B	11.	A
2.	B	12.	B
3.	B	13.	A
4.	D	14.	C
5.	A	15.	B
6.	C	16.	C
7.	D	17.	A
8.	B	18.	D
9.	A	19.	C
10.	C	20.	A

21.	B
22.	B
23.	C
24.	B
25.	C

EXAMINATION SECTION
TEST 1

DIRECTIONS: Each question or incomplete statement is followed by several suggested answers or completions. Select the one that BEST answers the question or completes the statement. *PRINT THE LETTER OF THE CORRECT ANSWER IN THE SPACE AT THE RIGHT.*

1. In performing a systems study, the analyst may find it necessary to prepare an accurate record of working statistics from departmental forms, questionnaires, and information gleaned in interviews.
   Which one of the following statements dealing with the statistical part of the study is the MOST valid?

   A. The emphasis of every survey is data collection.
   B. Data should not be represented in narrative form.
   C. The statistical report should include the titles of personnel required for each processing task.
   D. In gathering facts, the objective of a systems study should be the primary consideration

2. The most direct method of obtaining information about activities in the area under study is by observation. There are several general rules for an analyst that are essential for observing and being accepted as an observer.
   The one of the following statements relating to this aspect of an analyst's responsibility that is most valid in the initial phase is that the analyst should NOT

   A. limit himself to observing only; he may criticize operations and methods
   B. prepare himself for what he is about to observe
   C. obtain permission of the department's management to actually perform some of the clerical tasks himself
   D. offer views of impending charges regarding new staff requirements, equipment, or procedures

3. The active concern of the systems analyst is the study and documentation of what he observes as it exists. Before attempting the actual study and documentation, the analyst should comply with certain generally accepted procedures.
   Of the following, the step the analyst should *generally lake* FIRST is to

   A. define the problem and prepare a statement of objectives
   B. confer with the project director concerning persons to be interviewed
   C. accumulate data from all available sources within the area under study
   D. meet with operations managers to enlist their cooperation

4. During the course of any systems study, the analyst will have to gather some statistics if the operation model is to be realistic and meaningful.
   With respect to the statistical report part of the study, it is MOST valid to say that

A. it must follow a standard format since there should be no variation from one study to the next
B. the primary factor to be considered is the volume of work in the departmental unit at each stage of completion
C. only variations that occur during peak and slow periods should be recorded
D. unless deadlines in the departmental units studied by the analyst occur constantly, they should not be taken into account

5. In systems analysis, the interview is one of the analyst's major sources of information. In conducting an interview, he should strive for immediate rapport with the operations manager or department head with whom he deals.
With respect to his responsibility in this area, it is considered LEAST appropriate for the analyst to

   A. explain the full background of the study and the scope of the investigation
   B. emphasize the importance of achieving the stated objectives and review the plan of the project
   C. assume that the attitudes of the workers are less important than those of the executives
   D. request the manager's assistance in the form of questions, suggestions, and general cooperation

6. Large, complex endeavors often take a long time to implement. The following statements relate to long lead times imposed by large-scale endeavors.
Select the one usually considered to be LEAST valid.

   A. Where there are external sponsors who provide funds or political support, they should be provided with some demonstration of what is being accomplished.
   B. Long lead times simplify planning and diminish the threat of obsolescence by assuring that objectives will be updated by the time the project is nearing completion.
   C. During the period when no tangible results are forthcoming, techniques must be found to assess progress.
   D. Employees, particularly scientific personnel, should feel a sense of accomplishment or they may shy away from research which involves long-term commitments.

7. In traditional management theory, administrators are expected to collect and weigh facts and probabilities, make an optimal decision and see that it is carried out.
In the management of large-scale development projects, such a clear sequence of action is *generally* NOT possible because of

   A. their limited duration
   B. the static and fixed balance of power among interest groups
   C. continuous suppression of new facts
   D. constantly changing constraints and pressures

Questions 8-10.

DIRECTIONS: One of the most valuable parts of the systems package is the systems flowchart, a technique that aids understanding of the work flow. A flowchart should depict all the intricacies of the work flow from start to finish in order to give the onlooker a solid picture at a glance. The table below contains symbols used by the analyst in flowcharting. In answering Questions 8 through 10, refer to the following figures.

Figure I — rectangle
Figure II — rectangle with one angled corner
Figure III — rectangle with curved bottom
Figure IV — circle with tail
Figure V — parallelogram
Figure VI — diamond
Figure VII — hexagon
Figure VIII — wavy rectangle
Figure IX — rectangle with curved top
Figure X — trapezoid
Figure XI — curved rectangle
Figure XII — circle
Figure XIII — square (filled border)

8. The symbol that is COMMONLY used to specify clerical procedures which are not essential to the main processing function and yet are part of the overall procedure is represented by Figure

   A. III   B. VI   C. XII   D. XIII

9. An analyst wishes to designate the following activities:
   File reports; Calculate average; Attach labels.
   The MOST APPROPRIATE symbol to use is represented by Figure

   A. V   B. VI   C. VII   D. II

10. A *Report, Journal,* or *Record* should be represented by Figure

    A. I   B. III   C. IX   D. XI

Question 11.

DIRECTIONS: The following figures are often used in program and systems flowcharting.

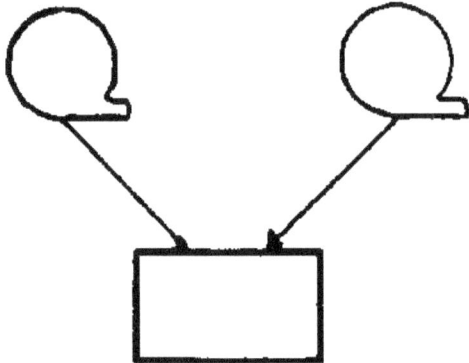

11. The above figures represent

    A. two storage discs incorporated in a processing function
    B. two report papers to be put in a cabinet in chronological order
    C. two transmittal tapes—both externally generated—routed to a vault
    D. an auxiliary operation involving two sequential decisions

12. When research and analysis of government programs, e.g., pest control, drug rehabilitation, etc., is sponsored and conducted within a government unit, the scope of the analysis should *generally* be _____ the scope of the authority of the manager to whom the analyst is responsible.

    A. less than
    B. less than or equal to
    C. greater than or equal to
    D. greater than

13. In recent years, there has been an increasing emphasis on outputs—the goods and services that a program produces. This emphasis on outputs imposes an information requirement. The one of the following which would MOST likely NOT be considered output information in a hospital or health care program is the

    A. number of patients cared for
    B. number of days patients were hospitalized
    C. budgeted monies for hospital beds
    D. quality of the service

14. Which one of the following statements pertaining to management information systems is generally considered to be LEAST valid?

    A. A management information system is a network of related subsystems developed according to an integrated scheme for evaluating the activities of an agency.
    B. A management information system specifies the content and format, the preparation and integration of information for all various functions within an agency that will best satisfy needs at various levels of management.
    C. To operate a successful management information system, an agency will require a complex electronic computer installation.
    D. The five elements which compose a management information system are: data input, files, data processing, procedures, and data output.

15. In the field of records management, electronic equipment is being used to handle office paperwork or data processing. With respect to such use, of the following, it is MOST valid to say that

    A. electronic equipment is not making great strides in the achievement of speed and economy in office paperwork
    B. electronic equipment accelerates the rate at which office paperwork is completed
    C. paperwork problems can be completely solved through mechanization
    D. introduction of electronic data processing equipment cuts down on the paper consumed in office processes

16. A reports control program evaluates the reporting requirements of top management so that reviews can be made of the existing reporting system to determine its adequacy. Of the following statements pertaining to reports control, which is the MOST likely to be characteristic of such a program?

    A. Only the exception will be reported
    B. Preparation of daily reports will be promoted
    C. Executives will not delegate responsibility for preparing reports
    D. Normal conditions are reported

17. Which of the following types of work measurement techniques requires the HIGHEST degree of training and skill of technicians and supervisors and is MOST likely to involve the HIGHEST original cost?

    A. Work sampling
    B. Predetermined time standards
    C. The time study (stopwatch timing)
    D. Employee reporting

18. Which of the following types of work measurement techniques *generally* requires the LEAST amount of time to measure and establish standards?

    A. Work sampling
    B. Predetermined time standards
    C. The time study (stopwatch timing)
    D. Employee reporting

19. Assume that you, as an analyst, have been assigned to formally organize small work groups within a city department to perform a special project. After studying the project, you find you must choose between two possible approaches—either task teams or highly functionalized groups.
    What would be one of the advantages of choosing the task-team approach over the highly functionalized organization?

    A. Detailed, centralized planning would be encouraged.
    B. Indifference to city goals and restrictions on output would be lessened.
    C. Work would be divided into very specialized areas.
    D. Superiors would be primarily concerned with seeing that subordinates do not deviate from the project.

20. In systems theory, there is a *what-if* method of treating uncertainty that explores the effect on the alternatives of environmental change. This method is generally referred to as _____ analysis.

   A. sensitivity
   B. contingency
   C. a fortiori
   D. systems

KEY (CORRECT ANSWERS)

1. D
2. D
3. A
4. B
5. C
6. B
7. D
8. D
9. A
10. B
11. A
12. B
13. C
14. C
15. B
16. A
17. B
18. A
19. B
20. B

TEST 2

DIRECTIONS: Each question or incomplete statement is followed by several suggested answers or completions. Select the one that BEST answers the question or completes the statement. *PRINT THE LETTER OF THE CORRECT ANSWER IN THE SPACE AT THE RIGHT.*

1. Which of the following systems exists at the strategic level of an organization?

   A. Decision support system (DSS)
   B. Executive support system (ESS)
   C. Knowledge work system (KWS)
   D. Management information system (MIS)

2. The functions of knowledge workers in an organization generally include each of the following EXCEPT

   A. updating knowledge
   B. managing documentation of knowledge
   C. serving as internal consultants
   D. acting as change agents

3. Which of the following is not a management benefit associated with end-user development of information systems?

   A. Reduced application backlog
   B. Increased user satisfaction
   C. Simplified testing and documentation procedures
   D. Improved requirements determination

4. Assume that an analyst is preparing an analysis of a departmental program. His investigation leads him to a potential problem relating to the program. The analyst thinks the potential problem is so serious that he cannot rely on preventive actions to remove the cause or significantly reduce the probability of its occurrence.
   Of the following, the MOST appropriate way for the analyst to promptly handle this serious matter described above would be to

   A. apply systematic afterthought to the achievement of objectives by analysis of the problem
   B. compare actual performance with the expected standard of performance
   C. prepare contingency actions to be adopted immediately if the problem does occur
   D. identify, locate, and describe the deviation from the standard

5. Assume that an analyst is directed to investigate a problem relating to organizational behavior in his agency and to prepare a report thereon. After reviewing the preliminary draft, his superior cautions him to overcome his tendency to misuse and overgeneralize his interpretation of existing knowledge.
   Which one of the following statements appearing in the draft is MOST *usually* considered to be a common distortion of behavioral science knowledge?

   A. Pay—even incentive pay—isn't very important anymore.
   B. There are nonrational aspects to people's behavior.
   C. The informal system exerts much control over organizational participants.
   D. Employees have many motives.

Questions 6-10.

DIRECTIONS: Each of Questions 6 through 10 consists of a statement which contains one word that is incorrectly used because it is not in keeping with the meaning that the quotation is evidently intended to convey. Determine which word is incorrectly used. Then select from the words lettered A, B, C, or D the word which, when substituted for the incorrectly used word, would BEST help to convey the meaning of the statement.

6. While the utilization of cost-benefit analysis in decision-making processes should be encouraged, it must be well understood that there are many limitations on the constraints of the analysis. One must be cautioned against using cost-benefit procedures automatically and blindly. Still, society will almost certainly be better off with the application of cost-benefit methods than it would be without them. As some authorities aptly point out, an important advantage of a cost-benefit study is that it forces those responsible to quantify costs and benefits as far as possible rather than rest content with vague qualitative judgments or personal hunches. Also, such an analysis has the very valuable byproduct of causing questions to be asked which would otherwise not have been raised. Finally, even if cost-benefit analysis cannot give the right answer, it can sometimes play the purely negative role of screening projects and rejecting those answers which are obviously less promising.

   A. precise
   B. externally
   C. applicability
   D. unresponsiveness

7. The programming method used by the government should attempt to assess the costs and benefits of individual projects, in comparison with private and other public alternatives. The program, then, consists of the most meritorious projects that the budget will design. Meritorious projects excluded from the budget provide arguments for increasing its size. There are difficulties inherent in the specific project approach. The attempt is to apply profit criteria in public projects analogous to those used in evaluating private projects. This involves comparison of monetary values of present and future costs and benefits. But, in many important cases, such as highways, parkways, and bridges, the product of the government's investment does not directly enter the market economy. Consequently, evaluation requires imputation of market values. For example, the returns on a bridge have been estimated by attempting to value the time saved by users. Such measurements necessarily contain a strong, element of artificiality.

   A. annulled   B. expedient   C. accommodate   D. marginally

8. Consider the problem of budgeting for activities designed to alleviate poverty and rooted unemployment. Are skill retraining efforts better or worse investments than public works? Are they better or worse than subsidies or other special incentives to attract new industry? Or, at an even more fundamental level, is a dollar invested in an attempt to rehabilitate a mature, technologically displaced, educationally handicapped, unemployed man a better commitment than a comparable dollar invested in supporting the educational and technical preparation of his son for employment in a different line of work? The questions may look unreasonable, even unanswerable. But the fact is that they are implicitly answered in any budget decision in the defined problem area. The only subordinate issue is whether the answer rests on intuition and guess, or on a budget system that presents relevant information so organized as to contribute to rational analysis, planning, and decision-making.

   A. incomplete
   B. relevant
   C. significant
   D. speculate

9. Choices among health programs, on the basis of cost-benefit analysis, raise another set of ethical problems. Measuring discounted lifetime earnings does not reveal the value of alleviating pain and suffering; some diseases have a high death rate, others are debilitating, others are merely uncomfortable. In general, choices among health and education programs that are predicated on discounted lifetime earnings will structure the choice against those who have low earnings, those whose earnings will materialize only at some future point in time, or those whose participation in the labor force is limited. It may be an appropriate economic policy to reduce expenditures in areas that maximize the future level of national income. But the maximization of social welfare may dictate attention to considerations, such as equality of opportunity, that transcend the limitations of values defined in such narrow terms.

    A. concentrate   B. divergent   C. enforcing   D. favorably

10. Without defined and time-phased objectives, it is difficult to be critical of administrative performance. To level a charge of waste or malperformance at the managers of a public program is, of course, one of the more popular pastimes of any administration's loyal opposition. But it is a rare experience to find such a charge documented by the kind of precise cost-effectiveness measures that are the common test of the quality of management performance in a well-run organization. Those who take a professional view of management responsibility are even more concerned about the acceptance of the kind of information that would enable a manager to assess the progress and quality of his own performance and, as appropriate, to initiate corrective action before outside criticism can even start.

    A. absence   B. rebut   C. withdraw   D. impeded

11. What is the relationship between the cost of inputs and the value of outputs when the results obtained from a program can be measured in money? _____ ratio.

    A. Value administrative-cost   B. Break-even point
    C. Variable-direct   D. Cost-benefit

12. Some writers in the field of public expenditure have noted a disturbing tendency inherent in cost-benefit analysis. Which one of the following statements MOST accurately expresses their concern over the use of cost-benefit analysis? It

    A. encourages the attachment of monetary values to intangibles
    B. has a built-in neglect of measurable outcomes while emphasizing the nonmeasurable
    C. consciously exaggerates social values and overstates political values
    D. encourages emphasis of those costs and benefits that cannot be measured rather than those that can

13. In private industry, budgetary control begins logically with an estimate of sales and the income therefrom.
    Of the following, the term used in government which is MOST analogous to that of sales in private industry is

    A. borrowed funds   B. the amount appropriated
    C. general overhead   D. surplus funds

14. When constructing graphs of causally related variables, how should the variables be placed to conform to conventional use?

    A. The independent variable should be placed on the vertical axis and the dependent variable on the horizontal axis.
    B. The dependent variable should be placed on the vertical axis and the independent variable on the horizontal axis.
    C. Independent variables should be placed on both axes.
    D. Dependent variables should be placed on both axes.

Questions 15-18.

DIRECTIONS: Answer Questions 15 through 18 on the basis of the following graph describing the output of computer operators.

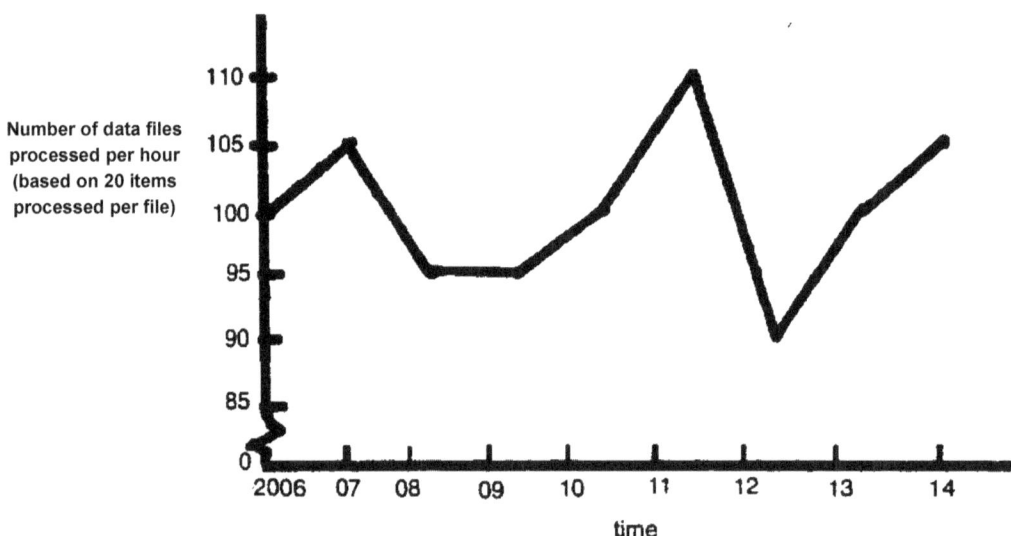

15. Of the following, during what four-year period did the AVERAGE OUTPUT of computer operators *fall below* 100 data files per hour?

    A. 2007-10   B. 2008-11   C. 2010-13   D. 2011-14

16. The AVERAGE PERCENTAGE CHANGE in output over the previous year's output for the years 2009 to 2012 is MOST NEARLY

    A. 2   B. 0   C. -5   D. -7

17. The DIFFERENCE between the actual output for 2012 and the projected figure based upon the average increase from 2006 to 2011 is MOST NEARLY

    A. 18   B. 20   C. 22   D. 24

18. Assume that after constructing the above graph, you, an analyst, discovered that the average number of items processed per file in 2012 was 25 (instead of 20) because of the complex nature of the work performed during that period.
    The AVERAGE OUTPUT in files per hour for the period 2010 to 2013, expressed in terms of 20 items per file, would then be APPROXIMATELY

    A. 95   B. 100   C. 105   D. 110

19. Assume that Unit S's production fluctuated substantially from one year to another. In 2009, Unit S's production was 100% greater than in 2008; in 2010, it was 25% less than in 2009; and in 2011, it was 10% greater than in 2010. On the basis of this information, it is CORRECT to conclude that Unit S's production in 2011 exceeded its production in 2008 by

    A. 50%   B. 65%   C. 75%   D. 90%

20. Statistical sampling is often used in administrative operations primarily because it enables

    A. administrators to make staff selections
    B. decisions to be made based on mathematical and scientific fact
    C. courses of action to be determined by electronic data processing or computer programs
    D. useful predictions to be made from relatively small samples

KEY (CORRECT ANSWERS)

1. B
2. B
3. C
4. C
5. A

6. C
7. C
8. C
9. A
10. A

11. D
12. A
13. B
14. B
15. A

16. B
17. C
18. C
19. B
20. D

EXAMINATION SECTION
TEST 1

DIRECTIONS: Each question or incomplete statement is followed by several suggested answers or completions. Select the one that BEST answers the question or completes the statement. *PRINT THE LETTER OF THE CORRECT ANSWER IN THE SPACE AT THE RIGHT.*

1. A systems analyst is beginning interviews in an operational area where he is expected to make a complete analysis. At first glance, the operation has poor supervision, poor working conditions, low morale, staff shortages, and general opposition to change. The first interview with the section chief is not very helpful to the analyst in understanding the operation.
   Of the following, it would be BEST for the analyst to

   A. bypass the section chief and speak directly to the workers
   B. pressure the section chief into being more open with him
   C. explain to the section chief how the analysis can help him with some of his problems
   D. formulate alternate plans for general systems improvement on the basis of obvious faults in the operation

1.____

2. The user requests changes after a system has been substantially coded.
   As the systems analyst implementing the system, you should

   A. ignore the request; at this stage there is no way of making any changes in the system
   B. determine the importance and impact of each change; be sure that user and system management sign-offs on the proposed changes include a statement of impact
   C. grant the changes; any change not made may have great implications on the effectiveness of the completed system
   D. grant the change only on condition that you are relieved of any responsibility for the performance of the system or the impact of modification

2.____

3. After having initially trained workers of a user section in their new job tasks, it is BEST for you as a trainer to

   A. turn the group over completely to their regular supervisor for any further training
   B. follow up very closely to see that they are doing the work properly
   C. restrict any further contact with the group to those workers who seem to have the most difficulty
   D. begin your training role but make yourself unavailable as a consultant

3.____

4. Which of the following statements offers the BEST guideline in drawing up schedules for analysis and coding?

   A. If you break down the work assignments into small enough units, you should be able to make good estimates of the time necessary to complete the project.
   B. Put enough good analysts and coders on a project, and you can meet practically any deadline.
   C. In order to avoid the effects of Parkinson's Law (work expands to fill the time allotted), you should usually draw up a tight schedule.
   D. Additional time for unforeseen problems should be added to time estimates when trying to predict a relatively accurate final completion target date.

4.____

5. In replacing a manual system with an EDP system, the FIRST concern of the analyst in charge should be

    A. the overall framework of the new system
    B. the accuracy of the specific procedures
    C. correct definition and explanation of the instruments to be used
    D. cross-referencing between manual and EDP procedures

6. In the course of instructing a trainee in the operation of a machine, there comes a time when it is best to let the trainee make an initial trial under the instructor's direct supervision.
   This step in the learning sequence is *usually* IMMEDIATELY _____ of the machine.

    A. *before* the instructor demonstrates the operation
    B. *before* the instructor explains the purpose
    C. *after* the instructor demonstrates the operation
    D. *after* the instructor explains the purpose

7. Assume that a new EDP system is being installed for a division. The analyst observes suspicion and indifference in the user's staff toward the new project.
   Of the following, what is the BEST course of action to be taken?

    A. Arrange for transfers for the discontented workers
    B. Assign more work to the employees
    C. Develop greater competition among the workers and a stronger interest in management functions
    D. Educate the workers in the purposes and objectives of the project

8. While doing a systems study, an analyst often observes the activities in the area under study to clarify the jobs of the employees and the methods utilized in processing the work of the section.
   One general rule ESSENTIAL for observing and being accepted as an observer is to

    A. discuss the work being done in the area, giving frank criticism of current methods
    B. tell the employees the details of all possible changes
    C. avoid voicing criticism to the employees being observed
    D. avoid showing interest so as to maintain a formal distance from the employees

9. Assume that, in the course of making a feasibility study for the installation of an EDP system, older workers show extreme resistance to converting the manual system. The resistance takes the form of far-fetched reasons why EDP will not work in their situation.
   Of the following, the BEST course of action to take in dealing with these workers is to tell them

    A. that they are as good as the younger workers and should adapt well to EDP
    B. exactly what changes in their work will be made because of the change to EDP
    C. that their reasons for disliking EDP are ill-founded and that they have nothing to fear
    D. that the methods used in their unit will be adapted to their desires, if possible

10. As a supervisor, you have received a rather complicated set of instructions for a new project which is to begin immediately. Some of the instructions are confusing. Your FIRST step should be to

    A. attempt to clear up with your supervisor any ambiguities before beginning the project
    B. instruct your staff to get started on the project immediately while you try to clarify the instructions
    C. discuss the matter with other supervisors at your level to find out if they have received clarification
    D. figure out the instructions as best you can and provide firm guidelines for your subordinates on the basis of your own good judgment

10.____

11. During the course of your work on the development of a new system, you realize that there is a big difference between what you think is needed and what the head of your agency thinks is needed. The agency head does not have a technical background in computer work.
Your BEST course of action is to

    A. develop a system based on what the agency head thinks is needed
    B. create a system based on what you think is needed
    C. base your system on what you believe would be acceptable compromise between the two viewpoints
    D. discuss the differences between the two points of view with the agency head and abide by his decision

11.____

12. As part of the unit under your supervision, you have been assigned a recent college graduate who is learning computer systems analysis. Although he has had computer systems and programming courses in college, he appears to be slow in doing the analysis preparatory to designing a subsystem.
The BEST course of action for you to follow FIRST in dealing with this worker is to

    A. check the possibility of his reassignment to a unit that has less strenuous work demands
    B. reduce the size of the subsystem assigned to him so that he can finish his work with little assistance
    C. let him work at his own pace, but help him with any parts of the analysis that are especially troublesome
    D. remind him of the need for meeting production demands and threaten to terminate his employment if his production does not improve

12.____

13. While working on a system design, a systems analyst is told by the user that certain changes must be made that will affect the system specification.
Of the following, which method would you use to handle these changes?

    A. Establish a formal procedure, including an approval mechanism requiring sign-offs by user and systems management.
    B. Make changes as the requests are made since there is usually no need to consult management.
    C. Refuse to permit changes in specifications that will impact the project schedule.
    D. Permit changes in specifications to be handled informally if they do not substantially alter the cost of system implementation.

13.____

14. The BEST attitude for you to assume in conducting interviews with user staff during the preliminary analysis is to

    A. act superior; their increased respect will cause them to be more open with you
    B. try to gain the respect of the staff by giving them a great deal of technical information on computers
    C. be personal; exchange views on management innovations including the proposed computer installation
    D. get the staff involved in the study; let them know that the information they are supplying is important

15. Observation of work procedures is used for many purposes in the process of systems analysis.
    Which of the following represents a FAULTY purpose of observation in an analytic situation?
    To

    A. give the analyst an overall view of the flow of routine tasks
    B. identify workers who are performing poorly in a manual operation
    C. confirm information secured in an interview
    D. clarify information secured in written form

16. The input requirements of a new system are such that the workflow in a clerical division will have to radically change. The supervisor of the division has asked you to help him in the training and instruction of his staff.
    Your PRIMARY consideration in this task is to

    A. perform it as quickly as possible so as to promote a rapid readjustment
    B. concentrate on what you know best, the input requirements of the EDP system
    C. organize a thorough training course and help the supervisor reorganize the work assignments
    D. concentrate on those staff members who are reacting to the changeover in a negative emotional manner

17. On-the-job training is one of the most common methods used to teach the employees of a user section the skills necessary for job performance in a changeover from a manual system to an EDP system.
    Which of the following is *most* likely to be a DISADVANTAGE of this type of training?

    A. In most instances, on-the-job training is carried out with little or no planning, causing a lack of focus.
    B. The employee gains experience in the environment in which he will be working.
    C. Employees usually resent this type of training because they must learn from their own mistakes.
    D. After the employee has developed sufficient skills, the trainer must follow up to determine the results of the training.

18. Most of the analysts working under your supervision are consistently submitting sub-systems as ready for coding which actually have logical inconsistencies of one sort or another. You have called this to their attention but the problem persists.
Of the following, the BEST method of improving their performance is to

    A. constantly make them aware of the delays caused by incomplete analysis
    B. correct the deficiencies yourself before submitting subsystems to programmer
    C. encourage the analysts to do more exchanging of flow charts among themselves so that they can find each other's mistakes
    D. reduce your criticism since it can be harmful to team productivity

19. A research technique which would be applied to determine the optimum number of window clerks or interviewers to have in an agency serving the public would MOST likely be the use of

    A. line of balance
    B. queuing theory
    C. simulation
    D. work sampling

20. The technique of work measurement in which the analyst observes the work at random times of the day is BEST termed

    A. indirect observation
    B. logging
    C. ratio delay
    D. wrist watch

21. A technique by which the supervisor or an assistant distributes a predetermined batch of work to the employees at periodic intervals of the day is generally BEST known as

    A. backlog control scheduling
    B. production control scheduling
    C. short interval scheduling
    D. workload balancing

22. If an analyst is required to recommend the selection of a machine for an office operation, he can BEST judge the expected output of a particular machine by pursuing which of the following courses of action?
Obtaining

    A. an actual test run of the machine in his office
    B. data from the manufacturer of the machine
    C. information on the percentage of working time the machine will be used
    D. the experience of actual users of similar machines elsewhere

23. Theoretically, an ideal organizational structure can be set up for each enterprise. In actual practice, the ideal organizational structure is seldom, if ever, obtained.
Of the following, the one that normally is of LEAST influence in determining the organizational structure is the

    A. existence of agreements and favors among members of the division
    B. funds available
    C. opinions and beliefs of top executives
    D. tendency of management to discard established forms in favor of new forms

24. An IMPORTANT aspect to keep in mind during the decision-making process is that 24.____
    A. all possible alternatives for attaining goals should be sought out and considered
    B. considering various alternatives only leads to confusion
    C. once a decision has been made it cannot be retracted
    D. there is only one correct method to reach any goal

25. Implementation of accountability requires 25.____
    A. a leader who will not hesitate to take punitive action
    B. an established system of communication from the bottom to the top
    C. explicit directives from leaders
    D. too much expense to justify it

KEY (CORRECT ANSWERS)

1. C	11. D
2. B	12. C
3. B	13. A
4. D	14. D
5. A	15. B
6. C	16. C
7. D	17. A
8. C	18. C
9. B	19. B
10. A	20. C

21. C
22. A
23. D
24. A
25. B

TEST 2

DIRECTIONS: Each question or incomplete statement is followed by several suggested answers or completions. Select the one that BEST answers the question or completes the statement. *PRINT THE LETTER OF THE CORRECT ANSWER IN THE SPACE AT THE RIGHT.*

1. Of the following, the MAJOR difference between systems and procedures analysis and work simplification is: 1.____

   A. The former complicates organization routine and the latter simplifies it
   B. The former is objective and the latter is subjective
   C. The former generally utilizes expert advice and the latter is a *do-it-yourself* improvement by supervisors and workers
   D. There is no difference other than in name

2. Systems development is concerned with providing   2.____

   A. a specific set of work procedures
   B. an overall framework to describe general relationships
   C. definitions of particular organizational functions
   D. organizational symbolism

3. Organizational systems and procedures should be   3.____

   A. developed as problems arise as no design can anticipate adequately the requirements of an organization
   B. developed jointly by experts in systems and procedures and the people who are responsible for implementing them
   C. developed solely by experts in systems and procedures
   D. eliminated whenever possible to save unnecessary expense

4. The CHIEF danger of a decentralized control system is that   4.____

   A. excessive reports and communications will be generated
   B. problem areas may not be detected readily
   C. the expense will become prohibitive
   D. this will result in too many *chiefs*

5. Of the following, management guides and controls clerical work PRINCIPALLY through   5.____

   A. close supervision and constant checking of personnel
   B. spot checking of clerical procedures
   C. strong sanctions for clerical supervisors
   D. the use of printed forms

6. Which of the following is MOST important before conducting fact-finding interviews?   6.____

   A. Becoming acquainted with all personnel to be interviewed
   B. Explaining the techniques you plan to use
   C. Explaining to the operating officials the purpose and scope of the study
   D. Orientation of the physical layout

7. Of the following, the one that is NOT essential in carrying out a comprehensive work improvement program is

   A. standards of performance
   B. supervisory training
   C. work count/task list
   D. work distribution chart

8. Which of the following control techniques is MOST useful on large, complex systems projects?
   A

   A. general work plan
   B. Gantt chart
   C. monthly progress report
   D. PERT chart

9. The action which is MOST effective in gaining acceptance of a study by the agency which is being studied is

   A. a directive from the agency head to install a study based on recommendations included in a report
   B. a lecture-type presentation following approval of the procedures
   C. a written procedure in narrative form covering the proposed system with visual presentations and discussions
   D. procedural charts showing the *before* and *after* situation, forms, steps, etc. to the employees affected

10. Which organizational principle is MOST closely related to procedural analysis and improvement?

    A. Duplication, overlapping, and conflict should be eliminated.
    B. Managerial authority should be clearly defined.
    C. The objectives of the organization should be clearly defined.
    D. Top management should be freed of burdensome detail.

11. Which one of the following is the MAJOR objective of operational audits?

    A. Detecting fraud
    B. Determining organizational problems
    C. Determining the number of personnel needed
    D. Recommending opportunities for improving operating and management practices

12. Of the following, the formalization of organizational structure is BEST achieved by

    A. a narrative description of the plan of organization
    B. functional charts
    C. job descriptions together with organizational charts
    D. multi-flow charts

13. Budget planning is MOST useful when it achieves

    A. cost control
    B. forecast of receipts
    C. performance review
    D. personnel reduction

14. The underlying principle of sound administration is to

    A. base administration on investigation of facts
    B. have plenty of resources available
    C. hire a strong administrator
    D. establish a broad policy

15. Although questionnaires are not the best survey tool the management analyst has to use, there are times when a good questionnaire can expedite the *fact-finding* phase of a management survey.
    Which of the following should be AVOIDED in the design and distribution of the questionnaire?

    A. Questions should be framed so that answers can be classified and tabulated for analysis.
    B. Those receiving the questionnaire must be knowledgeable enough to accurately provide the information desired.
    C. The questionnaire should enable the respondent to answer in a narrative manner.
    D. The questionnaire should require a minimum amount of writing.

16. The term that may be defined as a systematic analysis of all factors affecting work being done or all factors that will affect work to be done, in order to save effort, time or money is

    A. flow process charting
    B. work flow analysis
    C. work measurement
    D. work simplification

17. Generally, the LEAST important basic factor to be considered in developing office layout improvements is to locate

    A. office equipment, reference facilities, and files as close as practicable to those using them
    B. persons as close as practicable to the persons from whom they receive their work
    C. persons as close as practicable to windows and/or adequate ventilation
    D. persons who are friendly with each other close together to improve morale

18. Of the following, the one which is LEAST effective in reducing administrative costs is

    A. applying objective measurement techniques to determine the time required to perform a given task
    B. establishing budgets on the basis of historical performance data
    C. motivating supervisors and managers in the importance of cost reduction
    D. selecting the best method–manual, mechanical, or electronic–to process the essential work

19. *Fire-fighting* is a common expression in management terminology.
    Of the following, which BEST describes *fire-fighting* as an analyst's approach to solving paperwork problems?

    A. A complete review of all phases of the department's processing functions
    B. A studied determination of the proper equipment to process the work
    C. An analysis of each form that is being processed and the logical reasons for its processing
    D. The solution of problems as they arise, usually at the request of operating personnel

20. Assume that an analyst with a proven record of accomplishment on many projects is having difficulties on his present assignment.
    Of the following, the BEST course of action for his supervisor to take is to

    A. assume there is a personality conflict involved and transfer the analyst to another project
    B. give the analyst some time off
    C. review the nature of the project to determine whether or not the analyst is equipped to handle the assignment
    D. suggest that the analyst seek counseling

21. Downward communication from upper management to lower levels in an organization will often not be fully accepted at the lowest levels of an organization UNLESS high-level management

    A. communicates through several levels of mid-level management where the message can be properly modified and interpreted
    B. communicates directly with the level of the organization it wishes to reach, bypassing any intermediate levels
    C. first establishes an atmosphere in which upward communication is encouraged and listened to
    D. establishes penalties for non-compliance with its communications

22. A top-level manager sometimes has an inaccurate view of the actual lower-level operations of his agency, particularly of those operations which are not running well. Of the following, the MOST frequent cause of this is the

    A. general unconcern of top-level management with the way an agency actually operates
    B. tendency of the people at the lowest level in an agency to lie about their actual performance
    C. unwillingness of top level management to deal with unfavorable information when it is presented
    D. tendency of mid-level management to edit bad news and unpleasant information from reports directed to top management

23. In the conduct of productivity analyses, work measurement is a *useful* technique for

    A. substantiating executive decisions
    B. designing a research study
    C. developing performance yardsticks
    D. preparing a manual of procedure

24. What organizational concept is illustrated when a group is organized on an *ad hoc* basis to accomplish a specific goal?

    A. Functional teamwork
    B. Line/staff
    C. Task force
    D. Command

25. In order to give line personnel some insight into staff problems and vice versa, it has been suggested that line and staff assignments within a particular city agency be rotated. Which of the following criticisms would be MOST valid for OPPOSING such a proposal?

    A. Generally speaking, line and staff personnel have different perspectives on organizational structures which makes rotation in assignments extremely difficult.
    B. Since their educational backgrounds are often quite diverse, staff personnel are often at a disadvantage when serving in line assignments.
    C. Line personnel frequently resent having to perform the more difficult tasks that staff assignments entail.
    D. Serving in a rotating assignment may not necessarily provide the personnel with any significant degree of insight as anticipated.

KEY (CORRECT ANSWERS)

1.	C	11.	D
2.	B	12.	C
3.	B	13.	A
4.	B	14.	A
5.	D	15.	C
6.	C	16.	D
7.	B	17.	D
8.	D	18.	B
9.	C	19.	D
10.	A	20.	C

21. C
22. D
23. C
24. C
25. D

DOCUMENTS AND FORMS
PREPARING WRITTEN MATERIALS
EXAMINATION SECTION
TEST 1

DIRECTIONS: Each question or incomplete statement is followed by several suggested answers or completions. Select the one that BEST answers the question or completes the statement. *PRINT THE LETTER OF THE CORRECT ANSWER IN THE SPACE AT THE RIGHT.*

1. The office layout chart is a sketch of the physical arrangement of the office to which has been added the flow lines of the principal work performed there.
   Which one of the following states the BEST advantage of superimposing the work flow onto the desk layout?

   A. Lighting and acoustics can be improved.
   B. Line and staff relationships can be determined.
   C. Obvious misarrangements can be corrected.
   D. The number of delays can be determined.

   1.____

2. An advantage of the multiple process chart over the flow process chart is that the multiple process chart shows the

   A. individual worker's activity
   B. number of delays
   C. sequence of operations
   D. simultaneous flow of work in several departments

   2.____

3. Of the following, which is the MAJOR advantage of a microfilm record retention system?

   A. Filing can follow the terminal digit system.
   B. Retrieving documents from the files is faster.
   C. Significant space is saved in storing records.
   D. To read a microfilm record, a film reader is not necessary.

   3.____

4. Assume that you are in the process of eliminating unnecessary forms.
   The answer to which one of the following questions would be LEAST relevant?

   A. Could the information be obtained elsewhere?
   B. Is the form properly designed?
   C. Is the form used as intended?
   D. Is the purpose of the form essential to the operation?

   4.____

5. Use of color in forms adds to their cost. Sometimes, however, the use of color will greatly simplify procedure and more than pay for itself in time saved and errors eliminated.
   This is ESPECIALLY true when

   A. a form passes through many reviewers
   B. considerable sorting is required
   C. the form is other than a standard size
   D. the form will not be sent through the mail

   5.____

6. Of the following techniques, the one *generally* employed and considered BEST in forms design is to provide writing lines into boxes with captions printed in small type

   A. centered in the lower part of the box
   B. centered in the upper part of the box
   C. in the upper left-hand corner of the box
   D. in the lower right-hand corner of the box

6.___

7. Many forms authorities advocate the construction of a functional forms file or index. If such a file is set up, the MOST effective way of classifying forms for such an index is classification by

   A. department
   B. form number
   C. name or type of form
   D. subject to which the form applies

7.___

8. Of the following, the symbol as used in a systems flow chart denotes
   A. decision
   B. document
   C. manual operation
   D. process

8.___

9. Assume you are assigned to analyze the details of the procedures a clerk follows in order to complete filling out an invoice or a requisition. Your purpose is to simplify and shorten the procedure he has been trained to use.
   The BEST appropriate chart for this purpose would be the

   A. block flow diagram   B. flow process chart
   C. forms flow chart   D. work distribution chart

9.___

10. What *generally* is the PRINCIPAL objection to the use of form letters? The

    A. difficulty of developing a form letter to serve the purpose
    B. excessive time involved in selecting the proper form letter
    C. errors in selecting form letters
    D. impersonality of form letters

10.___

11. In process charting, the symbol which is used when conditions (except those which intentionally change the physical or chemical characteristics of the object) do not permit or require immediate performance, is

11.___

A. □   B. ○   C. ◗   D. ▽

12. Assume that you are making a study of a central headquarters office which processes claims received from a number of district offices. You notice the following problems: Some employees are usually busy, while others doing the same kind of work in the same grade have little to do; high level professional people frequently spend considerable time searching for files in the file room. Which of the following charts would be MOST useful to record and analyze the data needed to help solve these problems?

    A. Forms distribution chart
    B. Process chart
    C. Space layout chart
    D. Work distribution chart

13. Which of the following questions has the LEAST significant bearing on the analysis of the paperwork flow?

    A. How is the work brought into the department and how is it taken away?
    B. How many work stations are involved in processing the work within the department?
    C. Is the work received and removed in the proper quantity?
    D. Where is the supervisor's desk located in relationship to those he supervises?

14. Which of the following does NOT have significant bearing on the arrangement, sequence, and zoning of information into box captions? The

    A. layout of the source documents from which the information is taken
    B. logical flow of data
    C. needs of forms to be prepared from this form
    D. type of print to be employed

15. In determining the space requirements of a form and the size of the boxes to be used, PRIMARY consideration should be given to the

    A. distribution of the form
    B. method of entry, i.e., handwritten or machine, and type of machine
    C. number of copies
    D. number of items to be entered

16. Of the following, the BEST technique to follow when providing instructions for the completion and routing of a form is to

    A. imprint the instructions on the face of the form
    B. imprint the instructions on the back of the form
    C. provide a written procedure to accompany the form
    D. provide verbal instructions when issuing the form

17. A forms layout style where a separate space in the shape of a box is provided for each item of information requested and the caption or question for each item is shown in the upper left-hand corner of each box, is known as the

    A. box style
    B. check box style
    C. check list style
    D. check box and check list style

18. The BEST type of chart to use in showing the absolute movement or change of a continuous series of data over a period of time, such as changes in prices, employment or expenses, is *usually* a

A. bar chart B. line chart
C. multiple bar chart D. pie chart

19. In order to secure information on several specific points from all the tenants of a project, it has been suggested that a questionnaire be distributed to be completed and returned by the tenants.
The use of such a procedure is, *generally,*

   A. *desirable,* because it is a valuable means of building the cooperative relationship which should exist between tenants and management
   B. *desirable,* because it provides a written record of each tenant's reply
   C. *undesirable,* because distribution and collection of questionnaires is time-consuming
   D. *undesirable,* because it makes no provision for the expression of related information or viewpoints

20. A functional forms file is a collection of forms which are grouped by

   A. purpose   B. department   C. title   D. subject

21. All of the following are reasons to consult a records retention schedule EXCEPT one. Which one is that? To determine

   A. whether something should be filed
   B. how long something should stay in file
   C. who should be assigned to filing
   D. when something on file should be destroyed

22. Listed below are four of the steps in the process of preparing correspondence for filing. If they were to be put in logical sequence, the SECOND step would be

   A. preparing cross-reference sheets or cards
   B. coding the correspondence using a classification system
   C. sorting the correspondence in the order to be filed
   D. checking for follow-up action required and preparing a follow-up slip

23. New material added to a file folder should *usually* be inserted

   A. in the order of importance (the most important in front)
   B. in the order of importance (the most important in back)
   C. chronologically (most recent in front)
   D. chronologically (most recent in back)

24. An individual is looking for a name in the white pages of a telephone directory. Which of the following BEST describes the system of filing found there? A(n)

   A. alphabetic file   B. sequential file
   C. locator file   D. index file

25. The MAIN purpose of a tickler file is to

   A. help prevent overlooking matters that require future attention
   B. check on adequacy of past performance
   C. pinpoint responsibility for recurring daily tasks
   D. reduce the volume of material kept in general files

KEY (CORRECT ANSWERS)

1.	C	11.	C
2.	D	12.	D
3.	C	13.	D
4.	B	14.	D
5.	B	15.	B
6.	C	16.	A
7.	D	17.	A
8.	A	18.	B
9.	B	19.	B
10.	D	20.	A

21. C
22. A
23. C
24. A
25. A

TEST 2

1. A *good* record-keeping system includes all of the following procedures EXCEPT the

    A. filing of useless records
    B. destruction of certain files
    C. transferring of records from one type of file to another
    D. creation of inactive files

2. A new program is being set up for which certain new forms will be needed. You have been asked to design these forms.
Of the following, the FIRST step you should take in planning the forms is

    A. finding out the exact purpose for which each form will be used
    B. deciding what size of paper should be used for each form
    C. determining whether multiple copies will be needed for any of the forms
    D. setting up a new filing system to handle the new forms

3. Assume that your department is being moved to new and larger quarters, and that you have been asked to suggest an office layout for the central clerical office.
Of the following, your FIRST step in planning the new layout should *ordinarily* be to

    A. find out how much money has been budgeted for furniture and equipment
    B. make out *work-flow* and *traffic-flow* charts for the clerical operations
    C. measure each piece of furniture and equipment that is presently in use
    D. determine which files should be moved to a storage area or destroyed

4. In modern office layouts, screens and dividers are often used instead of walls to set off working groups. Advantages given for this approach have included *all* of the following EXCEPT

    A. more frequent communication between different working groups
    B. reduction in general noise level
    C. fewer objections from employees who are transferred to different groups
    D. cost savings from increased sharing of office equipment

5. Of the following, the CHIEF reason for moving less active material from active to inactive files is to

    A. dispose of material that no longer has any use
    B. keep the active files down to a manageable size
    C. make sure that no material over a year old remains in active files
    D. separate temporary records from permanent records

6. On a general organization chart, staff positions NORMALLY should be pictured

    A. directly above the line positions to which they report
    B. to the sides of the main flow lines
    C. within the box of the highest level subordinate positions pictured
    D. directly below the line positions which report to them

7. When an administrator is diagramming an office layout, of the following, his PRIMARY job, *generally*, should be to indicate the

   A. lighting intensities that will be required by each operation
   B. noise level that will be produced by the various equipment employed in the office
   C. direction of the work flow and the distance involved in each transfer
   D. durability of major pieces of office equipment currently in use or to be utilized

8. One common guideline or rule-of-thumb ratio for evaluating the efficiency of files is the number of records requested divided by the number of records filed.
Generally, if this ratio is very low, it would point MOST directly to the need for

   A. improving the indexing and coding system
   B. improving the charge-out procedures
   C. exploring the need for transferring records from active storage to the archives
   D. exploring the need to encourage employees to keep more records in their private files

9. The GREATEST percentage of money spent on preparing and keeping the usual records in an office, *generally*, is expended for which one of the following?

   A. Renting space in which to place the record-keeping equipment
   B. Paying salaries of record-preparing and record-keeping personnel
   C. Depreciation of purchased record-preparation and record-keeping equipment
   D. Paper and forms upon which to place the records

10. The MAXIMUM number of 2 3/4" x 4 1/4" size forms which may be obtained from two reams of 17" x 22" paper is

    A. 4,000   B. 8,000   C. 16,000   D. 32,000

11. Word processing computer applications (i.e. Microsoft Word) generally provide all of the following advantages as compared to electric word processors EXCEPT

    A. documents save to disk automatically
    B. ability to include customized graphs and charts in a document
    C. wider selection of available fonts
    D. easily customized page orientation

12. Generally, the actual floor space occupied by a standard letter-size office file cabinet, when closed, is, *most nearly*,

    A. 1/2 square foot   B. 3 square feet
    C. 7 square feet   D. 11 square feet

13. In general, the CHIEF economy of using multicopy forms is in

    A. the paper on which the form is printed
    B. printing the form
    C. employee time
    D. carbon paper

14. Suppose your supervisor has asked you to develop a form to record certain information needed. The FIRST thing you should do is to

    A. determine the type of data that will be recorded repeatedly, so that it can be pre-printed
    B. study the relationship of the form to the job to be accomplished, so that the form can be planned
    C. determine the information that will be recorded in the same place on each copy of the form, so that it can be used as a check
    D. find out who will be responsible for supplying the information so that space can be provided for their signatures

15. Of the following, which is usually the MOST important guideline in writing business letters? A letter should be

    A. neat
    B. written in a formalized style
    C. written in clear language intelligible to the reader
    D. written in the past tense

16. Suppose you are asked to edit a policy statement. You note that personal pronouns like *you*, *we*, and *I* are used freely.
    Which of the following statements BEST applies to this use of personal pronouns? It

    A. is proper usage because written business language should not be different from carefully spoken business language
    B. requires correction because it is ungrammatical
    C. is proper because it is clearer and has a warmer tone
    D. requires correction because policies should be expressed in an impersonal manner

17. Good business letters are coherent. To be *coherent* means to

    A. keep only one unifying idea in the message
    B. present the total message
    C. use simple, direct words for the message
    D. tie together the various ideas in the message

18. Proper division of a letter into paragraphs requires that the writer of business letters should, as much as possible, be sure that

    A. each paragraph is short
    B. each paragraph develops discussion of just one topic
    C. each paragraph repeats the theme of the total message
    D. there are at least two paragraphs for every message

19. An editor is given a letter with this initial paragraph *We have received your letter, which we read with interest, and we are happy to respond to your question. In fact, we talked with several people in our office to get ideas to send to you.*
    Which of the following is it MOST reasonable for the editor to conclude? The paragraph is

    A. concise
    B. communicating something of value
    C. unnecessary
    D. coherent

20. Suppose that one of your duties is to dictate responses to routine requests from the public for information. A letter writer asks for information which, as expressed in a one-sentence, explicit agency rule, cannot be given out to the public.
Of the following ways of answering the letter, which is the MOST efficient?

   A. Quote verbatim that section of the agency rules which prohibits giving this information to the public
   B. Without quoting the rule, explain why you cannot accede to the request and suggest alternative sources
   C. Describe how carefully the request was considered before classifying it as subject to the rule forbidding the issuance of such information
   D. Acknowledge receipt of the letter and advise that the requested information is not released to the public

21. Suppose you have been asked to write and to prepare for reproduction new departmental vacation leave regulations. After you have written the new regulations, all of which fit on one page, which one of the following would be the BEST method of reproducing 800 copies?

   A. An outside private printer, because you can best maintain confidentiality using this technique
   B. Using your own computer's printer/copier, because it is most convenient
   C. Giving the job to a coworker in another department who does this type of work more frequently, since the coworker is more familiar with the process
   D. Using a high-volume color copier, because it is fastest and of highest quality

22. The files in your office have been overcrowded and difficult to work with since you started working there. One day your supervisor is transferred and another assistant in your office decides to discard three drawers of the oldest materials.
For him to take this action is

   A. *desirable;* it will facilitate handling the more active materials
   B. *desirable;* no file should be removed from its point of origin
   C. *desirable;* there is no need to burden a new supervisor with unnecessary information
   D. *undesirable;* no file should be discarded without first noting what material has been discarded

23. You have been criticized by the general supervisor because of spelling errors in some of your typing. You have only copied the reports as written and you realize that the errors occurred in work given to you by your immediate supervisor.
Of the following, the BEST way for you to handle this situation is to

   A. tell the general supervisor that the spelling errors are your immediate supervisor's, not yours, because they occur only when you type his reports
   B. tell the general supervisor that you only type the reports as given to you, without indicating anyone
   C. inform your immediate supervisor that you have been unjustly criticized because of his spelling errors and politely request that he be more careful in the future
   D. use a dictionary whenever you have doubt regarding spelling

24. You have recently found several items misfiled. You believe that this occurred because a new assistant in your section has been making mistakes.
    The BEST course of action for you to take is to

    A. refile the material and say nothing about it
    B. send your supervisor an anonymous note of complaint about the filing errors
    C. show the errors to the new assistant and tell him why they are errors in filing
    D. tell your supervisor that the new assistant makes a lot of errors in filing

---

KEY (CORRECT ANSWERS)

1.	A	11.	A
2.	A	12.	B
3.	B	13.	C
4.	B	14.	B
5.	B	15.	C
6.	B	16.	D
7.	C	17.	D
8.	C	18.	B
9.	B	19.	C
10.	D	20.	A

21. D
22. D
23. D
24. C

PREPARING WRITTEN MATERIAL
EXAMINATION SECTION
TEST 1

DIRECTIONS: Each of the sentences in this test may be classified under one of the following four categories:
- A. *Incorrect* because of faulty grammar or sentence structure
- B. *Incorrect* because of faulty punctuation
- C. *Incorrect* because of faulty capitalization
- D. *Correct*

Examine each sentence carefully to determine under which of the above four options it is best classified. Then, in the space at the right, print the capital letter preceding the option which is the BEST of the four suggested above.

(Each incorrect sentence contains but one type of error. Consider a sentence to be correct if it contains none of the types of errors mentioned, even though there may be other correct ways of expressing the same thought.)

1. This fact, together with those brought out at the previous meeting, prove that the schedule is satisfactory to the employees.   1.____

2. Like many employees in scientific fields, the work of bookkeepers and accountants requires accuracy and neatness.   2.____

3. "What can I do for you," the secretary asked as she motioned to the visitor to take a seat.   3.____

4. Our representative, Mr. Charles will call on you next week to determine whether or not your claim has merit.   4.____

5. We expect you to return in the spring; please do not disappoint us.   5.____

6. Any supervisor, who disregards the just complaints of his subordinates, is remiss in the performance of his duty.   6.____

7. Because she took less than an hour for lunch is no reason for permitting her to leave before five o'clock.   7.____

8. "Miss Smith," said the supervisor, "Please arrange a meeting of the staff for two o'clock on Monday."   8.____

9. A private company's vacation and sick leave allowance usually differs considerably from a public agency.   9.____

10. Therefore, in order to increase the efficiency of operations in the department, a report on the recommended changes in procedures was presented to the departmental committee in charge of the program.   10.____

111

11. We told him to assign the work to whoever was available. 11._____

12. Since John was the most efficient of any other employee in the bureau, he received the highest service rating. 12._____

13. Only those members of the national organization who resided in the middle West attended the conference in Chicago. 13._____

14. The question of whether the office manager has as yet attained, or indeed can ever hope to secure professional status is one which has been discussed for years. 14._____

15. No one knew who to blame for the error which, we later discovered, resulted in a considerable loss of time. 15._____

KEY (CORRECT ANSWERS)

1.	A	6.	B	11.	D
2.	A	7.	A	12.	A
3.	B	8.	C	13.	C
4.	B	9.	A	14.	B
5.	D	10.	D	15.	A

TEST 2

DIRECTIONS: Each of the sentences in this test may be classified under one of the following four categories:
- A. *Incorrect* because of faulty grammar or sentence structure
- B. *Incorrect* because of faulty punctuation
- C. *Incorrect* because of faulty capitalization
- D. *Correct*

1. The National alliance of Businessmen is trying to persuade private businesses to hire youth in the summertime.   1.____

2. The supervisor who is on vacation, is in charge of processing vouchers.   2.____

3. The activity of the committee at its conferences is always stimulating.   3.____

4. After checking the addresses again, the letters went to the mailroom.   4.____

5. The director, as well as the employees, are interested in sharing the dividends.   5.____

KEY (CORRECT ANSWERS)

1. C
2. B
3. D
4. A
5. A

TEST 3

DIRECTIONS: In each of the following groups of sentences, one of the four sentences is faulty in grammar, punctuation, or capitalization. Select the INCORRECT sentence in each case.

1. A. Sailing down the bay was a thrilling experience for me.
   B. He was not consulted about your joining the club.
   C. This story is different than the one I told you yesterday.
   D. There is no doubt about his being the best player.

2. A. He maintains there is but one road to world peace.
   B. It is common knowledge that a child sees much he is not supposed to see.
   C. Much of the bitterness might have been avoided if arbitration had been resorted to earlier in the meeting.
   D. The man decided it would be advisable to marry a girl somewhat younger than him.

3. A. In this book, the incident I liked least is where the hero tries to put out the forest fire.
   B. Learning a foreign language will undoubtedly give a person a better understanding of his mother tongue.
   C. His actions made us wonder what he planned to do next.
   D. Because of the war, we were unable to travel during the summer vacation.

4. A. The class had no sooner become interested in the lesson than the dismissal bell rang.
   B. There is little agreement about the kind of world to be planned at the peace conference.
   C. "Today," said the teacher, "we shall read 'The Wind in the Willows,' I am sure you'll like it.
   D. The terms of the legal settlement of the family quarrel handicapped both sides for many years.

5. A. I was so surprised that I was not able to say a word.
   B. She is taller than any other member of the class.
   C. It would be much more preferable if you were never seen in his company.
   D. We had no choice but to excuse her for being late.

KEY (CORRECT ANSWERS)

1. C
2. D
3. A
4. C
5. C

TEST 4

DIRECTIONS: In each of the following groups of sentences, one of the four sentences is faulty in grammar, punctuation, or capitalization. Select the INCORRECT sentence in each case.

1. A. Please send me these data at the earliest opportunity.
   B. The loss of their material proved to be a severe handicap.
   C. My principal objection to this plan is that it is impracticable.
   D. The doll had laid in the rain for an hour and was ruined.

2. A. The garden scissors, left out all night in the rain, were in a badly rusted condition.
   B. The girls felt bad about the misunderstanding which had arisen
   C. Sitting near the campfire, the old man told John and I about many exciting adventures he had had.
   D. Neither of us is in a position to undertake a task of that magnitude.

3. A. The general concluded that one of the three roads would lead to the besieged city.
   B. The children didn't, as a rule, do hardly anything beyond what they were told to do.
   C. The reason the girl gave for her negligence was that she had acted on the spur of the moment.
   D. The daffodils and tulips look beautiful in that blue vase.

4. A. If I was ten years older, I should be interested in this work.
   B. Give the prize to whoever has drawn the best picture.
   C. When you have finished reading the book, take it back to the library.
   D. My drawing is as good as or better than yours.

5. A. He asked me whether the substance was animal or vegetable.
   B. An apple which is unripe should not be eaten by a child.
   C. That was an insult to me who am your friend.
   D. Some spy must of reported the matter to the enemy.

6. A. Limited time makes quoting the entire message impossible.
   B. Who did she say was going?
   C. The girls in your class have dressed more dolls this year than we.
   D. There was such a large amount of books on the floor that I couldn't find a place for my rocking chair.

7. A. What with his sleeplessness and his ill health, he was unable to assume any responsibility for the success of the meeting.
   B. If I had been born in February, I should be celebrating my birthday soon.
   C. In order to prevent breakage, she placed a sheet of paper between each of the plates when she packed them.
   D. After the spring shower, the violets smelled very sweet.

8. A. He had laid the book down very reluctantly before the end of the lesson.
    B. The dog, I am sorry to say, had lain on the bed all night.
    C. The cloth was first lain on a flat surface; then it was pressed with a hot iron.
    D. While we were in Florida, we lay in the sun until we were noticeably tanned.

    8.____

9. A. If John was in New York during the recent holiday season, I have no doubt he spent most of the time with his parents.
    B. How could he enjoy the television program; the dog was barking and the baby was crying.
    C. When the problem was explained to the class, he must have been asleep.
    D. She wished that her new dress were finished so that she could go to the party.

    9.____

10. A. The engine not only furnishes power but light and heat as well.
    B. You're aware that we've forgotten whose guilt was established, aren't you?
    C. Everybody knows that the woman made many sacrifices for her children.
    D. A man with his dog and gun is a familiar sight in this neighborhood.

    10.____

KEY (CORRECT ANSWERS)

1.	D	6.	D
2.	C	7.	B
3.	B	8.	C
4.	A	9.	B
5.	D	10.	A

TEST 5

DIRECTIONS: Each of Questions 1 through 5 consists of a sentence which may be classified appropriately under one of the following four categories:
  A. *Incorrect* because of faulty grammar
  B. *Incorrect* because of faulty punctuation
  C. *Incorrect* because of faulty spelling
  D. *Correct*

Examine each sentence carefully. Then, print in the space at the right the letter preceding the category which is the BEST of the four suggested above
(Note: Each incorrect sentence contains only one type of error. Consider a sentence correct if it contains no errors, although there may be other correct ways of writing the sentence.)

1. Of the two employees, the one in our office is the most efficient.   1.____

2. No one can apply or even understand, the new rules and regulations.   2.____

3. A large amount of supplies were stored in the empty office.   3.____

4. If an employee is occassionally asked to work overtime, he should do so willingly.   4.____

5. It is true that the new procedures are difficult to use but, we are certain that you will learn them quickly.   5.____

6. The office manager said that he did not know who would be given a large allotment under the new plan.   6.____

7. It was at the supervisor's request that the clerk agreed to postpone his vacation.   7.____

8. We do not believe that it is necessary for both he and the clerk to attend the conference.   8.____

9. All employees, who display perseverance, will be given adequate recognition.   9.____

10. He regrets that some of us employees are dissatisfied with our new assignments.   10.____

11. "Do you think that the raise was merited," asked the supervisor?   11.____

12. The new manual of procedure is a valuable supplament to our rules and regulations.   12.____

13. The typist admitted that she had attempted to pursuade the other employees to assist her in her work.   13.____

14. The supervisor asked that all amendments to the regulations be handled by   14._____
    you and I.

15. The custodian seen the boy who broke the window.   15._____

KEY (CORRECT ANSWERS)

1.	A	6.	D	11.	B
2.	B	7.	D	12.	C
3.	A	8.	A	13.	C
4.	C	9.	B	14.	A
5.	B	10.	D	15.	A

PREPARING WRITTEN MATERIAL

PARAGRAPH REARRANGEMENT
COMMENTARY

The sentences that follow are in scrambled order. You are to rearrange them in proper order and indicate the letter choice containing the correct answer at the space at the right.

Each group of sentences in this section is actually a paragraph presented in scrambled order. Each sentence in the group has a place in that paragraph; no sentence is to be left out. You are to read each group of sentences and decide upon the best order in which to put the sentences so as to form a well-organized paragraph.

The questions in this section measure the ability to solve a problem when all the facts relevant to its solution are not given.

More specifically, certain positions of responsibility and authority require the employee to discover connection between events sometimes, apparently, unrelated. In order to do this, the employee will find it necessary to correctly infer that unspecified events have probably occurred or are likely to occur. This ability becomes especially important when action must be taken on incomplete information.

Accordingly, these questions require competitors to choose among several suggested alternatives, each of which presents a different sequential arrangement of the events. Competitors must choose the MOST logical of the suggested sequences.

In order to do so, they may be required to draw on general knowledge to infer missing concepts or events that are essential to sequencing the given events. Competitors should be careful to infer only what is essential to the sequence. The plausibility of the wrong alternatives will always require the inclusion of unlikely events or of additional chains of events which are NOT essential to sequencing the given events.

It's very important to remember that you are looking for the best of the four possible choices, and that the best choice of all may not even be one of the answers you're given to choose from.

There is no one right way to solve these problems. Many people have found it helpful to first write out the order of the sentences, as they would have arranged them, on their scrap paper before looking at the possible answers. If their optimum answer is there, this can save them some time. If it isn't, this method can still give insight into solving the problem. Others find it most helpful to just go through each of the possible choices, contrasting each as they go along. You should use whatever method feels comfortable and works for you.

While most of these types of questions are not that difficult, we've added a higher percentage of the difficult type, just to give you more practice. Usually there are only one or two questions on this section that contain such subtle distinctions that you're unable to answer confidently. And you then may find yourself stuck deciding between two possible choices, neither of which you're sure about.

EXAMINATION SECTION
TEST 1

DIRECTIONS: The following groups of sentences need to be arranged in an order that makes sense. Select the letter preceding the sequence that represents the BEST sentence order. *PRINT THE LETTER OF THE CORRECT ANSWER IN THE SPACE AT THE RIGHT.*

1.
   I. The keyboard was purposely designed to be a little awkward to slow typists down.
   II. The arrangement of letters on the keyboard of a typewriter was not designed for the convenience of the typist.
   III. Fortunately, no one is suggesting that a new keyboard be designed right away.
   IV. If one were, we would have to learn to type all over again.
   V. The reason was that the early machines were slower than the typists and would jam easily.
   The CORRECT answer is:
   A. I, III, IV, II, V
   B. II, V, I, IV, III
   C. V, I, II, III, IV
   D. II, I, V, III, IV

   1.____

2.
   I. The majority of the new service jobs are part-time or low-paying.
   II. According to the U.S. Bureau of Labor Statistics, jobs in the service sector constitute 72% of all jobs in this country.
   III. If more and more workers receive less and less money, who will buy the goods and services needed to keep the economy going?
   IV. The service sector is by far the fastest growing part of the United States economy.
   V. Some economists look upon this trend with great concern.
   The CORRECT answer is:
   A. II, IV, I, V, III
   B. II, III, IV, I, V
   C. V, IV, II, III, I
   D. III, I, II, IV, V

   2.____

3.
   I. They can also affect one's endurance.
   II. This can stabilize blood sugar levels, and ensure that the brain is receiving a steady, constant, supply of glucose, so that one is *hitting on all cylinders* while taking the test.
   III. By food, we mean real food, not junk food or unhealthy snacks.
   IV. For this reason, it is important not to skip a meal, and to bring food with you to the exam.
   V. One's blood sugar levels can affect how clearly one is able to think and concentrate during an exam.
   The CORRECT answer is:
   A. V, IV, II, III, I
   B. V, II, I, IV, III
   C. V, I, IV, III, II
   D. V, IV, I, III, II

   3.____

4. I.   Those who are the embodiment of desire are absorbed in material quests, and those who are the embodiment of feeling are warriors who value power more than possession.
    II. These qualities are in everyone, but in different degrees.
    III. But those who value understanding yearn not for goods or victory, but for knowledge.
    IV. According to Plato, human behavior flows from three main sources: desire, emotion, and knowledge.
    V.   In the perfect state, the industrial forces would produce but not rule, the military would protect but not rule, and the forces of knowledge, the philosopher kings, would reign.
    The CORRECT answer is:
    A. IV, V, I, II, III   B. V, I, II, III, IV
    C. IV, III, II, I, V   D. IV, II, I, III, V

5. I.   Of the more than 26,000 tons of garbage produced daily in New York City, 12,000 tons arrive daily at Fresh Kills.
    II. In a month, enough garbage accumulates there to fill the Empire State Building.
    III. In 1937, the Supreme Court halted the practice of dumping the trash of New York City into the sea.
    IV. Although the garbage is compacted, in a few years the mounds of garbage at Fresh Kills will be the highest points south of Maine's Mount Desert Island on the Eastern Seaboard.
    V.   Instead, tugboats now pull barges of much of the trash to Staten Island and the largest landfill in the world, Fresh Kills.
    The CORRECT answer is:
    A. III, V, IV, I, II   B. III, V, II, IV, I
    C. III, V, I, II, IV   D. III, II, V, IV, I

6. I.   Communists rank equality very high, but freedom very low.
    II. Unlike communists, conservatives place a high value on freedom and a very low value on equality.
    III. A recent study demonstrated that one way to classify people's political beliefs is to look at the importance placed on two words: freedom and equality.
    IV. Thus, by demonstrating how members of these groups feel about the two words, the study has proved to be useful for political analysts in several European countries.
    V.   According to the study, socialists and liberals rank both freedom and equality very high, while fascists rate both very low.
    The CORRECT answer is:
    A. III, V, I, II, IV   B. V, IV, III, I, II
    C. III, V, IV, II, I   D. III, I, II, IV, V

7. I. "Can there be anything more amazing than this?"
    II. If the riddle is successfully answered, his dead brothers will be brought back to life.
    III. "Even though man sees those around him dying every day," says Dharmaraj, "he still believes and acts as if he were immortal."
    IV. "What is the cause of ceaseless wonder?" asks the Lord of the Lake.
    V. In the ancient epic, The Mahabharata, a riddle is asked of one of the Pandava brothers.
    The CORRECT answer is:
    A. V, II, I, IV, III
    B. V, IV, III, I, II
    C. V, II, IV, III, I
    D. V, II, IV, I, III

8. I. On the contrary, the two main theories—the cooperative (neoclassical) theory and the radical (labor theory)—clearly rest on very different assumptions, which have very different ethical overtones.
    II. The distribution of income is the primary factor in determining the relative levels of material well-being that different groups or individuals attain.
    III. Of all issues in economics, the distribution of income is one of the most controversial.
    IV. The neoclassical theory tends to support the existing income distribution (or minor changes), while the labor theory ends to support substantial changes in the way income is distributed.
    V. The intensity of the controversy reflects the fact that different economic theories are not purely neutral, *detached* theories with no ethical or moral implications.
    The CORRECT answer is:
    A. II, I, V, IV, III
    B. III, II, V, I, IV
    C. III, V, II, I, IV
    D. III, V, IV, I, II

9. I. The pool acts as a broker and ensures that the cheapest power gets used first.
    II. Every six seconds, the pool's computer monitors all of the generating stations in the state and decides which to ask for more power and which to cut back.
    III. The buying and selling of electrical power is handled by the New York Power Pool in Guilderland, New York.
    IV. This is to the advantage of both the buying and selling utilities.
    V. The pool began operation in 1970, and consists of the state's eight electric utilities.
    The CORRECT answer is:
    A. V, I, II, III, IV
    B. IV, II, I, III, V
    C. III, V, I, IV, II
    D. V, III, IV, II, I

10. I. Modern English is much simpler grammatically than Old English.
    II. Finnish grammar is very complicated; there are some fifteen cases, for example.
    III. Chinese, a very old language, may seem to be the exception, but it is the great number of characters/words that must be mastered that makes it so difficult to learn, not its grammar.
    IV. The newest literary language—that is, written as well as spoken—is Finish, whose literary roots go back only to about the middle of the nineteenth century.
    V. Contrary to popular belief, the longer a language is been in use the simpler its grammar—not the reverse.

    The CORRECT answer is:
    A. IV, I, II, III, V
    B. V, I, IV, II, III
    C. I, II, IV, III, V
    D. IV, II, III, I, V

KEY (CORRECT ANSWERS)

1. D   6. A
2. A   7. C
3. C   8. B
4. D   9. C
5. C   10. B

TEST 2

DIRECTIONS: This type of question tests your ability to recognize accurate paraphrasing, well-constructed paragraphs, and appropriate style and tone. It is important that the answer you select contains only the facts or concepts given in the original sentences. It is also important that you be aware of incomplete sentences, inappropriate transitions, unsupported opinions, incorrect usage, and illogical sentence order. Paragraphs that do not include all the necessary facts and concepts, that distort them, or that add new ones are not considered correct.

The format for this section may vary. Sometimes, long paragraphs are given, and emphasis is placed on style and organization. Our first five questions are of this type. Other times, the paragraphs are shorter, and there is less emphasis on style and more emphasis on accurate representation of information. Our second group of five questions are of this nature.

For each of Questions 1 through 10, select the paragraph that BEST expresses the ideas contained in the sentences above it. *PRINT THE LETTER OF THE CORRECT ANSWER IN THE SPACE AT THE RIGHT.*

1.
    I. Listening skills are very important for managers.
    II. Listening skills are not usually emphasized.
    III. Whenever managers are depicted in books, manuals or the media, they are always talking, never listening.
    IV. We'd like you to read the enclosed handout on listening skills and to try to consciously apply them this week.
    V. We guarantee they will improve the quality of your interactions.

    A. Unfortunately, listening skills are not usually emphasized for managers. Managers are always depicted as talking, never listening. We'd like you to read the enclosed handout on listening skills. Please try to apply these principles this week. If you do, we guarantee they will improve the quality of your interactions.
    B. The enclosed handout on listening skills will be important improving the quality of your interactions. We guarantee it. All you have to do is take sometime this week to read and to consciously try to apply the principles. Listening skills are very important for manages, but they are not usually emphasized. Whenever managers are depicted in books, manuals or the media, they are always talking, never listening.
    C. Listening well is one of the most important skills a manager can have, yet it's not usually given much attention. Think about any representation of managers in books, manuals, or in the media that you may have seen. They're always talking, never listening. We'd like you to read the enclosed handout on listening skills and consciously try to apply them the rest of the week. We guarantee you will see a difference in the quality of your interactions.

1.____

D. Effective listening, one very important tool in the effective manager's arsenal, is usually not emphasized enough. The usual depiction of managers in books, manuals or the media is one in which they are always talking, never listening. We'd like you to read the enclosed handout and consciously try to apply the information contained therein throughout the rest of the week. We feel sure that you will see a marked difference in the quality of your interactions.

2. I. Chekhov wrote three dramatic masterpieces which share certain themes and formats: <u>Uncle Vanya</u>, <u>The Cherry Orchard</u>, and <u>The Three Sisters</u>.
    II. They are primarily concerned with the passage of time and how this erodes human aspirations.
    III. The plays are haunted by the ghosts of the wasted life.
    IV. The characters are concerned with life's lesser problems; however, such as the inability to make decisions, loyalty to the wrong cause, and the inability to be clear.
    V. This results in sweet, almost aching, type of a sadness referred to as Chekhovian.

    A. Chekhov wrote three dramatic masterpieces: <u>Uncle Vanya</u>, <u>The Cherry Orchard</u>, and <u>The Three Sisters</u>. These masterpieces share certain themes and formats: the passage of time, how time erodes human aspirations, and the ghosts of wasted life. Each masterpiece is characterized by a sweet, almost aching, type of sadness that has become known as Chekhovian. The sweetness of this sadness hinges on the fact that it is not the great tragedies of life which are destroying these characters, but their minor flaws: indecisiveness, misplaced loyalty, unclarity.
    B. <u>The Cherry Orchard</u>, <u>Uncle Vanya</u>, and <u>The Three Sisters</u> are three dramatic masterpieces written by Chekhov that use similar formats to explore a common theme. Each is primarily concerned with the way that passing time wears down human aspirations, and each is haunted by the ghosts of the wasted life. The characters are shown struggling futilely with the lesser problems of life: indecisiveness, loyalty to the wrong cause, and the inability to be clear. These struggles create a mood of sweet, almost aching, sadness that has become known as Chekhovian.
    C. Chekhov's dramatic masterpieces are, along with <u>The Cherry Orchard</u>, <u>Uncle Vanya</u>, and <u>The Three Sisters</u>. These plays share certain thematic and formal similarities. They are concerned most of all with the passage of time and the way in which time erodes human aspirations. Each play is haunted by the specter of the wasted life. Chekhov's characters are caught, however, by life's lesser snares: indecisiveness, loyalty to the wrong cause, and unclarity. The characteristic mood is a sweet, almost aching type of sadness that has come to be known as Chekhovian.
    D. A Chekhovian mood is characterized by sweet, almost aching, sadness. The term comes from three dramatic tragedies by Chekhov which revolve around the sadness of a wasted life. The three masterpieces (<u>Uncle Vanya</u>, <u>The Three Sisters</u>, and <u>The Cherry Orchard</u>) share the same

2.____

theme and format. The plays are concerned with how the passage of time erodes human aspirations. They are peopled with characters who are struggling with life's lesser problems. These are people who are indecisive, loyal to the wrong causes, or are unable to make themselves clear.

3.
I. Movie previews have often helped producers decide which parts of movies they should take out or leave in.
II. The first 1933 preview of King Kong was very helpful to the producers because many people ran screaming from the theater and would not return when four men first attacked by Kong were eaten by giant spiders.
III. The 1950 premiere of Sunset Boulevard resulted in the filming of an entirely new beginning, and a delay of six months in the film's release.
IV. In the original opening scene, William Holden was in a morgue talking with thirty-six other "corpses" about the ways some of them had died.
V. When he began to tell them of his life with Gloria Swanson, the audience found this hilarious, instead of taking the scene seriously.

3. ____

A. Movie previews have often helped producers decide what parts of movies they should leave in or take out. For example, the first preview of King Kong in 1933 was very helpful. In one scene, four men were first attacked by Kong and then eaten by giant spiders. Many members of the audience ran screaming from the theater and would not return. The premiere of the 1950 film Sunset Boulevard was also very helpful. In the original opening scene, William Holden was in a morgue with thirty-six other "corpses," discussing the ways some of them had died. When he began to tell them of his life with Gloria Swanson, the audience found this hilarious. They were supposed to take the scene seriously. The result was a delay of six months in the release of the film while a new beginning was added.

B. Movie previews have often helped producers decide whether they should change various parts of a movie. After the 1933 preview of King Kong, a scene in which four men who had been attacked by Kong were eaten by giant spiders was taken out as many people ran screaming from the theater and would not return. The 1950 premiere of Sunset Boulevard also led to some changes. In the original opening scene, William Holden was in a morgue talking with thirty-six other "corpses" about the ways some of them had died. When he began to tell them of his life with Gloria Swanson, the audience found this hilarious, instead of taking the scene seriously.

C. What do Sunset Boulevard and King Kong have in common? Both show the value of using movie previews to test audience reaction. The first 1933 preview of King Kong showed that a scene showing four men being eaten by giant spiders after having been attacked by Kong was too frightening for many people. They ran screaming from the theater and couldn't be coaxed back. The 1950 premiere of Sunset Boulevard was also a scream, but not the kind the producers intended. The movie opens with William Holden lying in a morgue discussing the ways they had died with thirty-six other "corpses." When he began to tell them of his life with Gloria Swanson, the audience couldn't take him seriously. Their laughter caused a six-month delay while the beginning was rewritten.

D. Producers very often use movie previews to decide if changes are needed. The premiere of Sunset Boulevard in 1950 led to a new beginning and a six-month delay in film release. At the beginning, William Holden and thirty-six other "corpses" discuss the ways some of them died. Rather than taking this seriously, the audience thought it was hilarious when he began to tell them of his life with Gloria Swanson. The first 1933 preview of King Kong was very helpful for its producers because one scene so terrified the audience that many of them ran screaming from the theater and would not return. In this particular scene, four men who had first been attacked by Kong were eaten by giant spiders.

4.
I. It is common for supervisors to view employees as "things" to be manipulated.
II. This approach does not motivate employees, nor does the carrot-and-stick approach because employees often recognize these behaviors and resent them.
III. Supervisors can change these behaviors by using self-inquiry and persistence.
IV. The best managers genuinely respect those they work with, are supportive and helpful, and are interested in working as a team with those they supervise.
V. They disagree with the Golden Rule that says "he or she who has the gold makes the rules."

    A. Some managers act as if they think the Golden Rule means "he or she who has the gold makes the rules." They show disrespect to employees by seeing them as "things" to be manipulated. Obviously, this approach does not motivate employees any more than the carrot-and-stick approach motivates them. The employees are smart enough to spot these behaviors and resent them. On the other hand, the managers genuinely respect those they work with, are supportive and helpful, and are interested in working as a team. Self-inquiry and persistence can change even the former type of supervisor into the latter.

    B. Many supervisors all into the trap of viewing employees as "things" to be manipulated, or try to motivate them by using a carrot-and-stick approach. These methods do not motivate employees, who often recognize the behaviors and resent them. Supervisors can change these behaviors, however, by using self-inquiry and persistence. The best managers are supportive and helpful, and have genuine respect for those with whom they work. They are interested in working as a team with those they supervise. To them, the Golden Rule is not "he or she who has the gold makes the rules."

    C. Some supervisors see employees as "things" to be used or manipulated using a carrot-and-stick technique. These methods don't work. Employees often see through them and resent them. A supervisor who wants to change may do so. The techniques of self-inquiry and persistence can be used to turn him or her into the type of supervisor who doesn't think the Golden Rule is "he or she who has the gold makes the rules." They may become like the best managers who treat those with whom they work with respect and give them help and support. These are the manager who know how to build a team.

D. Unfortunately, many supervisors act as if their employees are objects whose movements they can position at will. This mistaken belief has the same result as another popular motivational technique—the carrot-and-stick approach. Both attitudes can lead to the same result—resentment from those employees who recognize the behaviors for what they are. Supervisors who recognize these behaviors can change through the use of persistence and the use of self-inquiry. It's important to remember that the best managers respect their employees. They readily give necessary help and support and are interested in working as a team with those they supervise. To these managers, the Golden Rule is not "he or she who has the gold makes the rules."

5. I. The first half of the nineteenth century produced a group of pessimistic poets—Byron, De Musset, Heine, Pushkin, and Leopardi.
    II. It also produced a group of pessimistic composers—Schubert, Chopin, Schumann, and even the later Beethoven.
    III. Above all, in philosophy, there was the profoundly pessimistic philosopher, Schopenhauer.
    IV. The Revolution was dead, the Bourbons were restored, the feudal barons were reclaiming their land, and progress everywhere was being suppressed, as the great age was over.
    V. "I thank God," said Goethe, "that I am not young in so thoroughly finished a world."

5.____

   A. "I thank God," said Goethe, "that I am not young in so thoroughly finished a world." The Revolution was dead, the Bourbons were restored, the feudal barons were reclaiming their land, and progress everywhere was being suppressed. The first half of the nineteenth century produced a group of pessimistic poets: Byron, De Musset, Heine, Pushkin, and Leopardi. It also produced pessimistic composers: Schubert, Chopin, Schumann. Although Beethoven came later, he fits into this group, too. Finally and above all, it also produced a profoundly pessimistic philosopher, Schopenhauer. The great age was over.
   B. The first half of the nineteenth century produced a group of pessimistic poets: Byron, De Musset, Heine, Pushkin, and Leopardi. It produced a group of pessimistic composers: Schubert, Chopin, Schumann, and even the later Beethoven. Above all, it produced a profoundly pessimistic philosopher, Schopenhauer. For each of these men, the great age was over. The Revolution was dead, and the Bourbons were restored. The feudal barons were reclaiming their land, and progress everywhere was being suppressed.

C. The great age was over. The Revolution was dead—the Bourbons were restored, and the feudal barons were reclaiming their land. Progress everywhere was being suppressed. Out of this climate came a profound pessimism. Poets, like Byron, De Musset, Heine, Pushkin, and Leopardi; composers, like Schubert, Chopin, Schumann, and even the later Beethoven; and above all, a profoundly pessimistic philosopher, Schopenauer. This pessimism which arose in the first half of the nineteenth century is illustrated by these words of Goethe, "I thank God that I am not young in so thoroughly finished a world."

D. The first half of the nineteenth century produced a group of pessimistic poets, Byron, De Musset, Heine, Pushkin, and Leopardi—and a group of pessimistic composers, Schubert, Chopin, Schumann, and the later Beethoven. Above it all, it produced a profoundly pessimistic philosopher, Schopenhauer. The great age was over. The Revolution was dead, the Bourbons were restored, the feudal barons were reclaiming their land, and progress everywhere was being suppressed. "I thank God," said Goethe, "that I am not young in so thoroughly finished a world."

6. I. A new manager sometimes may feel insecure about his or her competence in the new position.
    II. The new manager may then exhibit defensive or arrogant behavior towards those one supervises, or the new manager may direct overly flattering behavior toward one's new supervisor.

    A. Sometimes, a new manager may feel insecure about his or her ability to perform well in this new position. The insecurity may lead him or her to treat others differently. He or she may display arrogant or defensive behavior towards those he or she supervises, or be overly flattering to his or her new supervisor.
    B. A new manager may sometimes feel insecure about his or her ability to perform well in the new position. He or she may then become arrogant, defensive, or overly flattering towards those he or she works with.
    C. There are times when a new manager may be insecure about how well he or she can perform in the new job. The new manager may also behave defensive or act in an arrogant way towards those he or she supervises, or overly flatter his or her boss.
    D. Sometimes a new manager may feel insecure about his or her ability to perform well in the new position. He or she may then display arrogant or defensive behavior towards those they supervise, or become overly flattering towards their supervisors.

6.____

7. I. It is possible to eliminate unwanted behavior by bringing it under stimulus control—tying the behavior to a cue, and then never, or rarely, giving the cue.
    II. One trainer successfully used this method to keep an energetic young porpoise from coming out of her tank whenever she felt like it, which was potentially dangerous.
    III. Her trainer taught her to do it for a reward, in response to a hand signal, and then rarely gave the signal.

7.____

A. Unwanted behavior can be eliminated by tying the behavior to a cue, and then never, or rarely, giving the cue. This is called stimulus control. One trainer was able to use this method to keep an energetic young porpoise from coming out of her tank by teaching her to come out for a reward in response to a hand signal, and then rarely giving the signal.
B. Stimulus control can be used to eliminate unwanted behavior. In this method, behavior is tied to a cue, and then the cue is rarely, if ever, given. One trainer was able to successfully use stimulus control to keep an energetic young porpoise from coming out of her tank whenever she felt like it—a potentially dangerous practice. She taught the porpoise to come out for a reward when she gave a hand signal, and then rarely gave the signal.
C. It is possible to eliminate behavior that is undesirable by bringing it under stimulus control by tying behavior to a signal, and then rarely giving the signal. One trainer successfully used this method to keep an energetic porpoise from coming out of her tank, a potentially dangerous situation. Her trainer taught the porpoise to do it for a reward, in response to a hand signal, and then would rarely give the signal.
D. By using stimulus control, it is possible to eliminate unwanted behavior by tying the behavior to a cue, and then rarely or never give the cue. One trainer was able to use this method to successfully stop a young porpoise from coming out of her tank whenever she felt like it. To curb this potentially dangerous practice, the porpoise was taught by the trainer to come out of the tank for a reward, in response to a hand signal, and then rarely given the signal.

8. I. There is a great deal of concern over the safety of commercial trucks, caused by their greatly increased role in serious accidents since federal deregulation in 1981.
   II. Recently, 60 percent of trucks in New York and Connecticut and 70 percent of trucks in Maryland randomly stopped by state troopers failed safety inspections.
   III. Sixteen states in the United States require no training at all for truck drivers.

   A. Since federal deregulation in 1981, there has been a great deal of concern over the safety of commercial trucks, and their greatly increased role in serious accidents. Recently, 60 percent of trucks in New York and Connecticut, and 70 percent of trucks in Maryland failed safety inspections. Sixteen states in the United States require no training at all for truck drivers.
   B. There is a great deal of concern over the safety of commercial trucks since federal deregulation in 1981. Their role in serious accidents has greatly increased. Recently, 60 percent of trucks randomly stopped in Connecticut and New York and 70 percent in Maryland failed safety inspections conducted by state troopers. Sixteen states in the United States provide no training at all for truck drivers.
   C. Commercial trucks have a greatly increased role in serious accidents since federal deregulation in 1981. This has led to a great deal of concern.

Recently, 70 percent of trucks in Maryland and 60 percent of trucks in New York and Connecticut failed inspection of those that were randomly stopped by state troopers. Sixteen states in the United States require no training for all truck drivers.

   D. Since federal deregulation in 1981, the role that commercial trucks have played in serious accidents has greatly increased, and this has led to a great deal of concern. Recently, 60 percent of trucks in New York and Connecticut, and 70 percent of trucks in Maryland randomly stopped by state troopers failed safety inspections. Sixteen states in the U.S. don't require any training for truck drivers.

9.
  I. No matter how much some people have, they still feel unsatisfied and want more, or want to keep what they have forever.
  II. One recent television documentary showed several people flying from New York to Paris for a one-day shopping spree to buy platinum earrings, because they were bored.
  III. In Brazil, some people were ordering coffins that cost a minimum of $45,000 and are equipping them with deluxe stereos, televisions, and other graveyard necessities.

  A. Some people, despite having a great deal, still feel unsatisfied and want more, or think they can keep what they have forever. One recent documentary on television showed several people enroute from Paris to New York for a one day shopping spree to buy platinum earrings, because they were bored. Some people in Brazil are even ordering coffins equipped with such graveyard necessities as deluxe stereos and televisions. The price of the coffins start at $45,000.
  B. No matter how much some people have, they may feel unsatisfied. This leads them to want more, or to want to keep what they have forever. Recently, a television documentary depicting several people flying from New York to Paris for a one day shopping spree to buy platinum earrings. They were bored. Some people in Brazil are ordering coffins that cost at least $45,000 and come equipped with deluxe televisions, stereos and other necessary graveyard items.
  C. Some people will be dissatisfied no matter how much they have. They may want more, or they may want to keep what they have forever. One recent television documentary showed several people, motivated by boredom, jetting from New York to Paris for a one-day shopping spree to buy platinum earrings. In Brazil, some people are ordering coffins equipped with deluxe stereos, televisions and other graveyard necessities. The minimum price for these coffins—$45,000.
  D. Some people are never satisfied. No matter how much they have they still want more, or think they can keep what they have forever. One television documentary recently showed several people flying from New York to Paris for the day to buy platinum earrings because they were bored. In Brazil, some people are ordering coffins that cost $45,000 and are equipped with deluxe stereos, televisions and other graveyard necessities.

9 (#2)

10.   I. A television signal or video signal has three parts.
    II. Its parts are the black-and-white portion, the color portion, and the synchronizing (sync) pulses, which keep the picture stable.
    III. Each video source, whether it's a camera or a video-cassette recorder contains its own generator of these synchronizing pulses to accompany the picture that it's sending in order to keep it steady and straight.
    IV. In order to produce a clean recording, a video-cassette recorder must "lock-up" to the sync pulses that are part of the video it is trying to record, and this effort may be very noticeable if the device does not have gunlock.

10.____

    A. There are three parts to a television or video signal: the black-and-white part, the color part, and the synchronizing (sync) pulses, which keep the picture stable. Whether it's a video-cassette recorder or a camera, each video source contains its own pulse that synchronizes and generates the picture it's sending in order to keep it straight and steady. A video-cassette recorder must "lock up" to the sync pulses that are part of the video it's trying to record. If the device doesn't have gunlock, this effort must be very noticeable.
    B. A video signal or television is comprised of three parts: the black-and-white portion, the color portion, and the sync (synchronizing) pulses, which keep the picture stable. Whether it's a camera or a video-cassette recorder, each video source contains its own generator of these synchronizing pulses. These accompany the picture that it's sending in order to keep it straight and steady. A video-cassette recorder must "lock up" to the sync pulses that are part of the video it is trying to record in order to produce a clean recording. This effort may be very noticeable if the device does not have gunlock.
    C. There are three parts to a television or video signal: the color portion, the black-and-white portion, and the sync (synchronizing pulses). These keep the picture stable. Each video source, whether it's a video-cassette recorder or a camera, generates these synchronizing pulses accompanying the picture it's sending in order to keep it straight and steady. If a clean recording is to be produced, a video-cassette recorder must store the sync pulses that are part of the video it is trying to record. This effort may not be noticeable if the device does not have gunlock.
    D. A television signal or video signal has three parts: the black-and-white portion, the color portion, and the synchronizing (sync) pulses. It's the sync pulses which keep the picture stable, which accompany it and keep it steady and straight. Whether it's a camera or a video-cassette recorder, each video source contains its own generator of these synchronizing pulses. To produce a clean recording, a video-cassette recorder must "lock up" to the sync pulses that are part of the video it is trying to record. If the device does not have gunlock, this effort may be very noticeable.

KEY (CORRECT ANSWERS)

1. C 6. A
2. B 7. B
3. A 8. D
4. B 9. C
5. D 10. D

PHILOSOPHY, PRINCIPLES, PRACTICES, AND TECHNICS OF SUPERVISION, ADMINISTRATION, MANAGEMENT, AND ORGANIZATION

TABLE OF CONTENTS

	Page
MEANING OF SUPERVISION	1
THE OLD AND THE NEW SUPERVISION	1
THE EIGHT (8) BASIC PRINCIPLES OF THE NEW SUPERVISION	1
I. Principle of Responsibility	1
II. Principle of Authority	2
III. Principle of Self-Growth	2
IV. Principle of Individual Worth	2
V. Principle of Creative Leadership	2
VI. Principle of Success and Failure	2
VII. Principle of Science	3
VIII. Principle of Cooperation	3
WHAT IS ADMINISTRATION?	3
I. Practices Commonly Classed as "Supervisory"	3
II. Practices Commonly Classed as "Administrative"	3
III. Practices Commonly Classed as Both "Supervisory" and "Administrative"	4
RESPONSIBILITIES OF THE SUPERVISOR	4
COMPETENCIES OF THE SUPERVISOR	4
THE PROFESSIONAL SUPERVISOR-EMPLOYEE RELATIONSHIP	4
MINI-TEXT IN SUPERVISION, ADMINISTRATION, MANAGEMENT, AND ORGANIZATION	5
I. Brief Highlights	5
A. Levels of Management	6
B. What the Supervisor Must Learn	6
C. A Definition of Supervision	6
D. Elements of the Team Concept	6
E. Principles of Organization	6
F. The Four Important Parts of Every Job	7
G. Principles of Delegation	7
H. Principles of Effective Communications	7
I. Principles of Work Improvement	7
J. Areas of Job Improvement	7
K. Seven Key Points in Making Improvements	8

L.	Corrective Techniques for Job Improvement	8
M.	A Planning Checklist	8
N.	Five Characteristics of Good Directions	9
O.	Types of Directions	9
P.	Controls	9
Q.	Orienting the New Employee	9
R.	Checklist for Orienting New Employees	9
S.	Principles of Learning	10
T.	Causes of Poor Performance	10
U.	Four Major Steps in On-the-Job Instructions	10
V.	Employees Want Five Things	10
W.	Some Don'ts in Regard to Praise	11
X.	How to Gain Your Workers' Confidence	11
Y.	Sources of Employee Problems	11
Z.	The Supervisor's Key to Discipline	11
AA.	Five Important Processes of Management	12
BB.	When the Supervisor Fails to Plan	12
CC.	Fourteen General Principles of Management	12
DD.	Change	12

II. Brief Topical Summaries — 13
    A. Who/What is the Supervisor? — 13
    B. The Sociology of Work — 13
    C. Principles and Practices of Supervision — 14
    D. Dynamic Leadership — 14
    E. Processes for Solving Problems — 15
    F. Training for Results — 15
    G. Health, Safety, and Accident Prevention — 16
    H. Equal Employment Opportunity — 16
    I. Improving Communications — 16
    J. Self-Development — 17
    K. Teaching and Training — 17
        1. The Teaching Process — 17
            a. Preparation — 17
            b. Presentation — 18
            c. Summary — 18
            d. Application — 18
            e. Evaluation — 18
        2. Teaching Methods — 18
            a. Lecture — 18
            b. Discussion — 18
            c. Demonstration — 19
            d. Performance — 19
            e. Which Method to Use — 19

PHILOSOPHY, PRINCIPLES, PRACTICES, AND TECHNICS
OF
SUPERVISION, ADMINISTRATION, MANAGEMENT, AND ORGANIZATION

MEANING OF SUPERVISION

The extension of the democratic philosophy has been accompanied by an extension in the scope of supervision. Modern leaders and supervisors no longer think of supervision in the narrow sense of being confined chiefly to visiting employees, supplying materials, or rating the staff. They regard supervision as being intimately related to all the concerned agencies of society, they speak of the supervisor's function in terms of "growth," rather than the "improvement" of employees.

This modern concept of supervision may be defined as follows: Supervision is leadership and the development of leadership within groups which are cooperatively engaged in inspection, research, training, guidance, and evaluation.

THE OLD AND THE NEW SUPERVISION

TRADITIONAL
1. Inspection
2. Focused on the employee
3. Visitation
4. Random and haphazard
5. Imposed and authoritarian
6. One person usually

MODERN
1. Study and analysis
2. Focused on aims, materials, methods, supervisors, employees, environment
3. Demonstrations, intervisitation, workshops, directed reading, bulletins, etc.
4. Definitely organized and planned (scientific)
5. Cooperative and democratic
6. Many persons involved (creative)

THE EIGHT (8) BASIC PRINCIPLES OF THE NEW SUPERVISION

I. Principle of Responsibility
   Authority to act and responsibility for acting must be joined.
   A. If you give responsibility, give authority.
   B. Define employee duties clearly.
   C. Protect employees from criticism by others.
   D. Recognize the rights as well as obligations of employees.
   E. Achieve the aims of a democratic society insofar as it is possible within the area of your work.
   F. Establish a situation favorable to training and learning.
   G. Accept ultimate responsibility for everything done in your section, unit, office, division, department.
   H. Good administration and good supervision are inseparable.

II. Principle of Authority
   The success of the supervisor is measured by the extent to which the power of authority is not used.
   A. Exercise simplicity and informality in supervision
   B. Use the simplest machinery of supervision
   C. If it is good for the organization as a whole, it is probably justified.
   D. Seldom be arbitrary or authoritative.
   E. Do not base your work on the power of position or of personality.
   F. Permit and encourage the free expression of opinions.

III. Principle of Self-Growth
   The success of the supervisor is measured by the extent to which, and the speed with which, he is no longer needed.
   A. Base criticism on principles, not on specifics.
   B. Point out higher activities to employees.
   C. Train for self-thinking by employees to meet new situations.
   D. Stimulate initiative, self-reliance, and individual responsibility
   E. Concentrate on stimulating the growth of employees rather than on removing defects.

IV. Principle of Individual Worth
   Respect for the individual is a paramount consideration in supervision.
   A. Be human and sympathetic in dealing with employees.
   B. Don't nag about things to be done.
   C. Recognize the individual differences among employees and seek opportunities to permit best expression of each personality.

V. Principle of Creative Leadership
   The best supervision is that which is not apparent to the employee.
   A. Stimulate, don't drive employees to creative action.
   B. Emphasize doing good things.
   C. Encourage employees to do what they do best.
   D. Do not be too greatly concerned with details of subject or method.
   E. Do not be concerned exclusively with immediate problems and activities.
   F. Reveal higher activities and make them both desired and maximally possible.
   G. Determine procedures in the light of each situation but see that these are derived from a sound basic philosophy.
   H. Aid, inspire, and lead so as to liberate the creative spirit latent in all good employees.

VI. Principle of Success and Failure
   There are no unsuccessful employees, only unsuccessful supervisors who have failed to give proper leadership.
   A. Adapt suggestions to the capacities, attitudes, and prejudices of employees.
   B. Be gradual, be progressive, be persistent.
   C. Help the employee find the general principle; have the employee apply his own problem to the general principle.
   D. Give adequate appreciation for good work and honest effort.
   E. Anticipate employee difficulties and help to prevent them.
   F. Encourage employees to do the desirable things they will do anyway.
   G. Judge your supervision by the results it secures.

VII. Principle of Science
Successful supervision is scientific, objective, and experimental. It is based on facts, not on prejudices.
   A. Be cumulative in results.
   B. Never divorce your suggestions from the goals of training.
   C. Don't be impatient of results.
   D. Keep all matters on a professional, not a personal, level.
   E. Do not be concerned exclusively with immediate problems and activities.
   F. Use objective means of determining achievement and rating where possible.

VIII. Principle of Cooperation
Supervision is a cooperative enterprise between supervisor and employee.
   A. Begin with conditions as they are.
   B. Ask opinions of all involved when formulating policies.
   C. Organization is as good as its weakest link.
   D. Let employees help to determine policies and department programs.
   E. Be approachable and accessible—physically and mentally.
   F. Develop pleasant social relationships.

WHAT IS ADMINISTRATION

Administration is concerned with providing the environment, the material facilities, and the operational procedures that will promote the maximum growth and development of supervisors and employees. (Organization is an aspect and a concomitant of administration.)

There is no sharp line of demarcation between supervision and administration; these functions are intimately interrelated and, often, overlapping. They are complementary activities.

I. Practices Commonly Classed as "Supervisory"
   A. Conducting employees' conferences
   B. Visiting sections, units, offices, divisions, departments
   C. Arranging for demonstrations
   D. Examining plans
   E. Suggesting professional reading
   F. Interpreting bulletins
   G. Recommending in-service training courses
   H. Encouraging experimentation
   I. Appraising employee morale
   J. Providing for intervisitation

II. Practices Commonly Classified as "Administrative"
   A. Management of the office
   B. Arrangement of schedules for extra duties
   C. Assignment of rooms or areas
   D. Distribution of supplies
   E. Keeping records and reports
   F. Care of audio-visual materials
   G. Keeping inventory records
   H. Checking record cards and books

    I.   Programming special activities
    J.   Checking on the attendance and punctuality of employees

III. Practices Commonly Classified as Both "Supervisory" and "Administrative"
    A.   Program construction
    B.   Testing or evaluating outcomes
    C.   Personnel accounting
    D.   Ordering instructional materials

RESPONSIBILITIES OF THE SUPERVISOR

A person employed in a supervisory capacity must constantly be able to improve his own efficiency and ability. He represent the employer to the employees and only continuous self-examination can make him a capable supervisor.

Leadership and training are the supervisor's responsibility. An efficient working unit is one in which the employees work with the supervisor. It is his job to bring out the best in his employees. He must always be relaxed, courteous, and calm in his association with his employees. Their feelings are important, and a harsh attitude does not develop the most efficient employees.

COMPETENCES OF THE SUPERVISOR

    I.   Complete knowledge of the duties and responsibilities of his position.
    II.   To be able to organize a job, plan ahead, and carry through.
    III.   To have self-confidence and initiative.
    IV.   To be able to handle the unexpected situation and make quick decisions.
    V.   To be able to properly train subordinates in the positions they are best suited for.
    VI.   To be able to keep good human relations among his subordinates.
    VII.   To be able to keep good human relations between his subordinates and himself and to earn their respect and trust.

THE PROFESSIONAL SUPERVISOR-EMPLOYEE RELATIONSHIP

There are two kinds of efficiency: one kind is only apparent and is produced in organizations through the exercise of mere discipline; this is but a simulation of the second, or true, efficiency which springs from spontaneous cooperation. If you are a manager, no matter how great or small your responsibility, it is your job, in the final analysis, to create and develop this involuntary cooperation among the people whom you supervise. For, no matter how powerful a combination of money, machines, and materials a company may have, this is a dead and sterile thing without a team of willing, thinking, and articulate people to guide it.

The following 21 points are presented as indicative of the exemplary basic relationship that should exist between supervisor and employee:

1. Each person wants to be liked and respected by his fellow employee and wants to be treated with consideration and respect by his superior.
2. The most competent employee will make an error. However, in a unit where good relations exist between the supervisor and his employees, tenseness and fear do not exist. Thus, errors are not hidden or covered up, and the efficiency of a unit is not impaired.

3. Subordinates resent rules, regulations, or orders that are unreasonable or unexplained.
4. Subordinates are quick to resent unfairness, harshness, injustices, and favoritism.
5. An employee will accept responsibility if he knows that he will be complimented for a job well done, and not too harshly chastised for failure; that his supervisor will check the cause of the failure, and, if it was the supervisor's fault, he will assume the blame therefore. If it was the employee's fault, his supervisor will explain the correct method or means of handling the responsibility.
6. An employee wants to receive credit for a suggestion he has made, that is used. If a suggestion cannot be used, the employee is entitled to an explanation. The supervisor should not say "no" and close the subject.
7. Fear and worry slow up a worker's ability. Poor working environment can impair his physical and mental health. A good supervisor avoids forceful methods, threats, and arguments to get a job done.
8. A forceful supervisor is able to train his employees individually and as a team, and is able to motivate them in the proper channels.
9. A mature supervisor is able to properly evaluate his subordinates and to keep them happy and satisfied.
10. A sensitive supervisor will never patronize his subordinates.
11. A worthy supervisor will respect his employees' confidences.
12. Definite and clear-cut responsibilities should be assigned to each executive.
13. Responsibility should always be coupled with corresponding authority.
14. No change should be made in the scope or responsibilities of a position without a definite understanding to that effect on the part of all persons concerned.
15. No executive or employee, occupying a single position in the organization, should be subject to definite orders from more than one source.
16. Orders should never be given to subordinates over the head of a responsible executive. Rather than do this, the officer in question should be supplanted.
17. Criticisms of subordinates should, whoever possible, be made privately, and in no case should a subordinate be criticized in the presence of executives or employees of equal or lower rank.
18. No dispute or difference between executives or employees as to authority or responsibilities should be considered too trivial for prompt and careful adjudication.
19. Promotions, wage changes, and disciplinary action should always be approved by the executive immediately superior to the one directly responsible.
20. No executive or employee should ever be required, or expected, to be at the same time an assistant to, and critic of, another.
21. Any executive whose work is subject to regular inspection should, wherever practicable, be given the assistance and facilities necessary to enable him to maintain an independent check of the quality of his work.

MINI-TEXT IN SUPERVISION, ADMINISTRATION, MANAGEMENT, AND ORGANIZATION

I. Brief Highlights

Listed concisely and sequentially are major headings and important data in the field for quick recall and review.

A. Levels of Management
Any organization of some size has several levels of management. In terms of a ladder, the levels are:

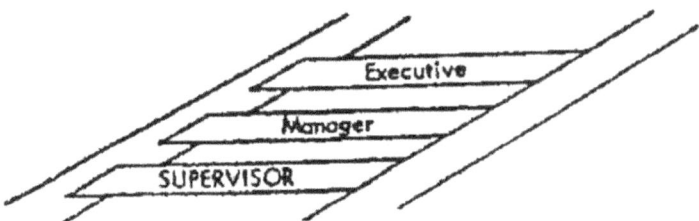

The first level is very important because it is the beginning point of management leadership.

B. What the Supervisor Must Learn
A supervisor must learn to:
1. Deal with people and their differences
2. Get the job done through people
3. Recognize the problems when they exist
4. Overcome obstacles to good performance
5. Evaluate the performance of people
6. Check his own performance in terms of accomplishment

C. A Definition of Supervisor
The term supervisor means any individual having authority, in the interests of the employer, to hire, transfer, suspend, lay-off, recall, promote, discharge, assign, reward, or discipline other employees or responsibility to direct them, or to adjust their grievances, or effectively to recommend such action, if, in connection with the foregoing, exercise of such authority is not of a merely routine or clerical nature but requires the use of independent judgment.

D. Elements of the Team Concept
What is involved in teamwork? The component parts are:
1. Members
2. A leader
3. Goals
4. Plans
5. Cooperation
6. Spirit

E. Principles of Organization
1. A team member must know what his job is.
2. Be sure that the nature and scope of a job are understood.
3. Authority and responsibility should be carefully spelled out.
4. A supervisor should be permitted to make the maximum number of decisions affecting his employees.
5. Employees should report to only one supervisor.
6. A supervisor should direct only as many employees as he can handle effectively.
7. An organization plan should be flexible.

8. Inspection and performance of work should be separate.
9. Organizational problems should receive immediate attention.
10. Assign work in line with ability and experience.

F. The Four Important Parts of Every Job
1. Inherent in every job is the *accountability* for results.
2. A second set of factors in every job is *responsibilities.*
3. Along with duties and responsibilities one must have the *authority* to act within certain limits without obtaining permission to proceed.
4. No job exists in a vacuum. The supervisor is surrounded by key *relationships.*

G. Principles of Delegation
Where work is delegated for the first time, the supervisor should think in terms of these questions:
1. Who is best qualified to do this?
2. Can an employee improve his abilities by doing this?
3. How long should an employee spend on this?
4. Are there any special problems for which he will need guidance?
5. How broad a delegation can I make?

H. Principles of Effective Communications
1. Determine the media.
2. To whom directed?
3. Identification and source authority.
4. Is communication understood?

I. Principles of Work Improvement
1. Most people usually do only the work which is assigned to them.
2. Workers are likely to fit assigned work into the time available to perform it.
3. A good workload usually stimulates output.
4. People usually do their best work when they know that results will be reviewed or inspected.
5. Employees usually feel that someone else is responsible for conditions of work, workplace layout, job methods, type of tools/equipment, and other such factors.
6. Employees are usually defensive about their job security.
7. Employees have natural resistance to change.
8. Employees can support or destroy a supervisor.
9. A supervisor usually earns the respect of his people through his personal example of diligence and efficiency.

J. Areas of Job Improvement
The areas of job improvement are quite numerous, but the most common ones which a supervisor can identify and utilize are:
1. Departmental layout
2. Flow of work
3. Workplace layout
4. Utilization of manpower
5. Work methods
6. Materials handling

7. Utilization
8. Motion economy

K. Seven Key Points in Making Improvements
1. Select the job to be improved
2. Study how it is being done now
3. Question the present method
4. Determine actions to be taken
5. Chart proposed method
6. Get approval and apply
7. Solicit worker participation

l. Corrective Techniques of Job Improvement
Specific Problems
1. Size of workload
2. Inability to meet schedules
3. Strain and fatigue
4. Improper use of men and skills
5. Waste, poor quality, unsafe conditions
6. Bottleneck conditions that hinder output
7. Poor utilization of equipment and machine
8. Efficiency and productivity of labor

General Improvement
1. Departmental layout
2. Flow of work
3. Work plan layout
4. Utilization of manpower
5. Work methods
6. Materials handling
7. Utilization of equipment
8. Motion economy

Corrective Techniques
1. Study with scale model
2. Flow chart study
3. Motion analysis
4. Comparison of units produced to standard allowance
5. Methods analysis
6. Flow chart and equipment study
7. Down time vs. running time
8. Motion analysis

M. A Planning Checklist
1. Objectives
2. Controls
3. Delegations
4. Communications
5. Resources
6. Manpower

7. Equipment
8. Supplies and materials
9. Utilization of time
10. Safety
11. Money
12. Work
13. Timing of improvements

N. Five Characteristics of Good Directions
In order to get results, directions must be:
1. Possible of accomplishment
2. Agreeable with worker interests
3. Related to mission
4. Planned and complete
5. Unmistakably clear

O. Types of Directions
1. Demands or direct orders
2. Requests
3. Suggestion or implication
4. volunteering

P. Controls
A typical listing of the overall areas in which the supervisor should establish controls might be:
1. Manpower
2. Materials
3. Quality of work
4. Quantity of work
5. Time
6. Space
7. Money
8. Methods

Q. Orienting the New Employee
1. Prepare for him
2. Welcome the new employee
3. Orientation for the job
4. Follow-up

R. Checklist for Orienting New Employees   Yes   No
1. Do you appreciate the feelings of new employees
   when they first report for work?   ___   ___
2. Are you aware of the fact that the new employee must
   make a big adjustment to his job?   ___   ___
3. Have you given him good reasons for liking the job and
   the organization?   ___   ___
4. Have you prepared for his first day on the job? ___   ___
5. Did you welcome him cordially and make him feel needed? ___ ___

	Yes	No

6. Did you establish rapport with him so that he feels free to talk and discuss matters with you? ____ ____
7. Did you explain his job to him and his relationship to you? ____ ____
8. Does he know that his work will be evaluated periodically on a basis that is fair and objective? ____ ____
9. Did you introduce him to his fellow workers in such a way that they are likely to accept him? ____ ____
10. Does he know what employee benefits he will receive? ____ ____
11. Does he understand the importance of being on the job and what to do if he must leave his duty station? ____ ____
12. Has he been impressed with the importance of accident prevention and safe practice? ____ ____
13. Does he generally know his way around the department? ____ ____
14. Is he under the guidance of a sponsor who will teach the right way of doing things? ____ ____
15. Do you plan to follow-up so that he will continue to adjust successfully to his job? ____ ____

S. Principles of Learning
1. Motivation
2. Demonstration or explanation
3. Practice

T. Causes of Poor Performance
1. Improper training for job
2. Wrong tools
3. Inadequate directions
4. Lack of supervisory follow-up
5. Poor communications
6. Lack of standards of performance
7. Wrong work habits
8. Low morale
9. Other

U. Four Major Steps in On-The-Job Instruction
1. Prepare the worker
2. Present the operation
3. Tryout performance
4. Follow-up

V. Employees Want Five Things
1. Security
2. Opportunity
3. Recognition
4. Inclusion
5. Expression

W. Some Don'ts in Regard to Praise
   1. Don't praise a person for something he hasn't done.
   2. Don't praise a person unless you can be sincere.
   3. Don't be sparing in praise just because your superior withholds it from you.
   4. Don't let too much time elapse between good performance and recognition of it

X. How to Gain Your Workers' Confidence
   Methods of developing confidence include such things as:
   1. Knowing the interests, habits, hobbies of employees
   2. Admitting your own inadequacies
   3. Sharing and telling of confidence in others
   4. Supporting people when they are in trouble
   5. Delegating matters that can be well handled
   6. Being frank and straightforward about problems and working conditions
   7. Encouraging others to bring their problems to you
   8. Taking action on problems which impede worker progress

Y. Sources of Employee Problems
   On-the-job causes might be such things as:
   1. A feeling that favoritism is exercised in assignments
   2. Assignment of overtime
   3. An undue amount of supervision
   4. Changing methods or systems
   5. Stealing of ideas or trade secrets
   6. Lack of interest in job
   7. Threat of reduction in force
   8. Ignorance or lack of communications
   9. Poor equipment
   10. Lack of knowing how supervisor feels toward employee
   11. Shift assignments

   Off-the-job problems might have to do with:
   1. Health
   2. Finances
   3. Housing
   4. Family

Z. The Supervisor's Key to Discipline
   There are several key points about discipline which the supervisor should keep in mind:
   1. Job discipline is one of the disciplines of life and is directed by the supervisor.
   2. It is more important to correct an employee fault than to fix blame for it.
   3. Employee performance is affected by problems both on the job and off.
   4. Sudden or abrupt changes in behavior can be indications of important employee problems.
   5. Problems should be dealt with as soon as possible after they are identified.
   6. The attitude of the supervisor may have more to do with solving problems than the techniques of problem solving.
   7. Correction of employee behavior should be resorted to only after the supervisor is sure that training or counseling will not be helpful.

8. Be sure to document your disciplinary actions.
9. Make sure that you are disciplining on the basis of facts rather than personal feelings.
10. Take each disciplinary step in order, being careful not to make snap judgments, or decisions based on impatience.

AA. Five Important Processes of Management
1. Planning
2. Organizing
3. Scheduling
4. Controlling
5. Motivating

BB. When the Supervisor Fails to Plan
1. Supervisor creates impression of not knowing his job
2. May lead to excessive overtime
3. Job runs itself—supervisor lacks control
4. Deadlines and appointments missed
5. Parts of the work go undone
6. Work interrupted by emergencies
7. Sets a bad example
8. Uneven workload creates peaks and valleys
9. Too much time on minor details at expense of more important tasks

CC. Fourteen General Principles of Management
1. Division of work
2. Authority and responsibility
3. Discipline
4. Unity of command
5. Unity of direction
6. Subordination of individual interest to general interest
7. Remuneration of personnel
8. Centralization
9. Scalar chain
10. Order
11. Equity
12. Stability of tenure of personnel
13. Initiative
14. Esprit de corps

DD. Change

Bringing about change is perhaps attempted more often, and yet less well understood, than anything else the supervisor does. How do people generally react to change? (People tend to resist change that is imposed upon them by other individuals or circumstances.

Change is characteristic of every situation. It is a part of every real endeavor where the efforts of people are concerned.

1. Why do people resist change?
   People may resist change because of:
   a. Fear of the unknown
   b. Implied criticism
   c. Unpleasant experiences in the past
   d. Fear of loss of status
   e. Threat to the ego
   f. Fear of loss of economic stability

2. How can we best overcome the resistance to change?
   In initiating change, take these steps:
   a. Get ready to sell
   b. Identify sources of help
   c. Anticipate objections
   d. Sell benefits
   e. Listen in depth
   f. Follow up

II. Brief Topical Summaries

   A. Who/What is the Supervisor?
      1. The supervisor is often called the "highest level employee and the lowest level manager."
      2. A supervisor is a member of both management and the work group. He acts as a bridge between the two.
      3. Most problems in supervision are in the area of human relations, or people problems.
      4. Employees expect: Respect, opportunity to learn and to advance, and a sense of belonging, and so forth.
      5. Supervisors are responsible for directing people and organizing work. Planning is of paramount importance.
      6. A position description is a set of duties and responsibilities inherent to a given position.
      7. It is important to keep the position description up-to-date and to provide each employee with his own copy.

   B. The Sociology of Work
      1. People are alike in many ways; however, each individual is unique.
      2. The supervisor is challenged in getting to know employee differences. Acquiring skills in evaluating individuals is an asset.
      3. Maintaining meaningful working relationships in the organization is of great importance.
      4. The supervisor has an obligation to help individuals to develop to their fullest potential.
      5. Job rotation on a planned basis helps to build versatility and to maintain interest and enthusiasm in work groups.
      6. Cross training (job rotation) provides backup skills.

14

7. The supervisor can help reduce tension by maintaining a sense of humor, providing guidance to employees, and by making reasonable and timely decisions. Employees respond favorably to working under reasonably predictable circumstances.
8. Change is characteristic of all managerial behavior. The supervisor must adjust to changes in procedures, new methods, technological changes, and to a number of new and sometimes challenging situations.
9. To overcome the natural tendency for people to resist change, the supervisor should become more skillful in initiating change.

C. Principles and Practices of Supervision
1. Employees should be required to answer to only one superior.
2. A supervisor can effectively direct only a limited number of employees, depending upon the complexity, variety, and proximity of the jobs involved.
3. The organizational chart presents the organization in graphic form. It reflects lines of authority and responsibility as well as interrelationships of units within the organization.
4. Distribution of work can be improved through an analysis using the "Work Distribution Chart."
5. The "Work Distribution Chart" reflects the division of work within a unit in understandable form.
6. When related tasks are given to an employee, he has a better chance of increasing his skills through training.
7. The individual who is given the responsibility for tasks must also be given the appropriate authority to insure adequate results.
8. The supervisor should delegate repetitive, routine work. Preparation of recurring reports, maintaining leave and attendance records are some examples.
9. Good discipline is essential to good task performance. Discipline is reflected in the actions of employees on the job in the absence of supervision.
10. Disciplinary action may have to be taken when the positive aspects of discipline have failed. Reprimand, warning, and suspension are examples of disciplinary action.
11. If a situation calls for a reprimand, be sure it is deserved and remember it is to be done in private.

D. Dynamic Leadership
1. A style is a personal method or manner of exerting influence.
2. Authoritarian leaders often see themselves as the source of power and authority.
3. The democratic leader often perceives the group as the source of authority and power.
4. Supervisors tend to do better when using the pattern of leadership that is most natural for them.
5. Social scientists suggest that the effective supervisor use the leadership style that best fits the problem or circumstances involved.
6. All four styles—telling, selling, consulting, joining—have their place. Using one does not preclude using the other at another time.

7. The theory X point of view assumes that the average person dislikes work, will avoid it whenever possible, and must be coerced to achieve organizational objectives.
8. The theory Y point of view assumes that the average person considers work to be a natural as play, and, when the individual is committed, he requires little supervision or direction to accomplish desired objectives.
9. The leader's basic assumptions concerning human behavior and human nature affect his actions, decisions, and other managerial practices.
10. Dissatisfaction among employees is often present, but difficult to isolate. The supervisor should seek to weaken dissatisfaction by keeping promises, being sincere and considerate, keeping employees informed, and so forth.
11. Constructive suggestions should be encouraged during the natural progress of the work.

E. Processes for Solving Problems
1. People find their daily tasks more meaningful and satisfying when they can improve them.
2. The causes of problems, or the key factors, are often hidden in the background. Ability to solve problems often involves the ability to isolate them from their backgrounds. There is some substance to the cliché that some persons "can't see the forest for the trees."
3. New procedures are often developed from old ones. Problems should be broken down into manageable parts. New ideas can be adapted from old one.
4. People think differently in problem-solving situations. Using a logical, patterned approach is often useful. One approach found to be useful includes these steps:
    a. Define the problem
    b. Establish objectives
    c. Get the facts
    d. Weigh and decide
    e. Take action
    f. Evaluate action

F. Training for Results
1. Participants respond best when they feel training is important to them.
2. The supervisor has responsibility for the training and development of those who report to him.
3. When training is delegated to others, great care must be exercised to insure the trainer has knowledge, aptitude, and interest for his work as a trainer.
4. Training (learning) of some type goes on continually. The most successful supervisor makes certain the learning contributes in a productive manner to operational goals.
5. New employees are particularly susceptible to training. Older employees facing new job situations require specific training, as well as having need for development and growth opportunities.
6. Training needs require continuous monitoring.
7. The training officer of an agency is a professional with a responsibility to assist supervisors in solving training problems.

8. Many of the self-development steps important to the supervisor's own growth are equally important to the development of peers and subordinates. Knowledge of these is important when the supervisor consults with others on development and growth opportunities.

G. Health, Safety, and Accident Prevention
1. Management-minded supervisors take appropriate measures to assist employees in maintaining health and in assuring safe practices in the work environment.
2. Effective safety training and practices help to avoid injury and accidents.
3. Safety should be a management goal. All infractions of safety which are observed should be corrected without exception.
4. Employees' safety attitude, training and instruction, provision of safe tools and equipment, supervision, and leadership are considered highly important factors which contribute to safety and which can be influenced directly by supervisors.
5. When accidents do occur, they should be investigated promptly for very important reasons, including the fact that information which is gained can be used to prevent accidents in the future.

H. Equal Employment Opportunity
1. The supervisor should endeavor to treat all employees fairly, without regard to religion, race, sex, or national origin.
2. Groups tend to reflect the attitude of the leader. Prejudice can be detected even in very subtle form. Supervisors must strive to create a feeling of mutual respect and confidence in every employee.
3. Complete utilization of all human resources is a national goal. Equitable consideration should be accorded women in the work force, minority-group members, the physically and mentally handicapped, and the older employee. The important question is: "Who can do the job?"
4. Training opportunities, recognition for performance, overtime assignments, promotional opportunities, and all other personnel actions are to be handled on an equitable basis.

I. Improving Communications
1. Communications is achieving understanding between the sender and the receiver of a message. It also means sharing information—the creation of understanding.
2. Communication is basic to all human activity. Words are means of conveying meanings; however, real meanings are in people.
3. There are very practical differences in the effectiveness of one-way, impersonal, and two-way communications. Words spoken face-to-face are better understood. Telephone conversations are effective, but lack the rapport of person-to-person exchanges. The whole person communicates.
4. Cooperation and communication in an organization go hand in hand. When there is a mutual respect between people, spelling out rules and procedures for communicating is unnecessary.
5. There are several barriers to effective communications. These include failure to listen with respect and understanding, lack of skill in feedback, and misinterpreting the meanings of words used by the speaker. It is also common

practice to listen to what we want to hear, and tune out things we do not want to hear.
6. Communication is management's chief problem. The supervisor should accept the challenge to communicate more effectively and to improve interagency and intra-agency communications.
7. The supervisor may often plan for and conduct meetings. The planning phase is critical and may determine the success or the failure of a meeting.
8. Speaking before groups usually requires extra effort. Stage fright may never disappear completely, but it can be controlled.

J. Self-Development
1. Every employee is responsible for his own self-development.
2. Toastmaster and toastmistress clubs offer opportunities to improve skills in oral communications.
3. Planning for one's own self-development is of vital importance. Supervisors know their own strengths and limitations better than anyone else.
4. Many opportunities are open to aid the supervisor in his developmental efforts, including job assignments; training opportunities, both governmental and non-governmental—to include universities and professional conferences and seminars.
5. Programmed instruction offers a means of studying at one's own rate.
6. Where difficulties may arise from a supervisor's being away from his work for training, he may participate in televised home study or correspondence courses to meet his self-development needs.

K. Teaching and Training
1. The Teaching Process
Teaching is encouraging and guiding the learning activities of students toward established goals. In most cases this process consists of five steps: preparation, presentation, summarization, evaluation, and application.

   a. Preparation
   Preparation is two-fold in nature; that of the supervisor and the employee. Preparation by the supervisor is absolutely essential to success. He must know what, when, where, how, and whom he will teach. Some of the factors that should be considered are:
   1) The objectives
   2) The materials needed
   3) The methods to be used
   4) Employee participation
   5) Employee interest
   6) Training aids
   7) Evaluation
   8) Summarization

   Employee preparation consists in preparing the employee to receive the material. Probably the most important single factor in the preparation of the employee is arousing and maintaining his interest. He must know the objectives of the training, why he is there, how the material can be used, and its importance to him.

18

b. Presentation
In presentation, have a carefully designed plan and follow it. The plan should be accurate and complete, yet flexible enough to meet situations as they arise. The method of presentation will be determined by the particular situation and objectives.

c. Summary
A summary should be made at the end of every training unit and program. In addition, there may be internal summaries depending on the nature of the material being taught. The important thing is that the trainee must always be able to understand how each part of the new material relates to the whole.

d. Application
The supervisor must arrange work so the employee will be given a chance to apply new knowledge or skills while the material is still clear in his mind and interest is high. The trainee does not really know whether he has learned the material until he has been given a chance to apply it. If the material is not applied, it loses most of its value.

e. Evaluation
The purpose of all training is to promote learning. To determine whether the training has been a success or failure, the supervisor must evaluate this learning.
In the broadest sense, evaluation includes all the devices, methods, skills, and techniques used by the supervisor to keep himself and the employees informed as to their progress toward the objectives they are pursuing. The extent to which the employee has mastered the knowledge, skills, and abilities, or changed his attitudes, as determined by the program objectives, is the extent to which instruction has succeeded or failed.
Evaluation should not be confined to the end of the lesson, day, or program but should be used continuously. We shall note later the way this relates to the rest of the teaching process.

2. Teaching Methods
A teaching method is a pattern of identifiable student and instructor activity used in presenting training material.
All supervisors are faced with the problem of deciding which method should be used at a given time.

a. Lecture
The lecture is direct oral presentation of material by the supervisor. The present trend is to place less emphasis on the trainer's activity and more on that of the trainee.

b. Discussion
Teaching by discussion or conference involves using questions and other techniques to arouse interest and focus attention upon certain areas, and by doing so creating a learning situation. This can be one of the most

valuable methods because it gives the employees an opportunity to express their ideas and pool their knowledge.

    c. Demonstration
The demonstration is used to teach how something works or how to do something. It can be used to show a principle or what the results of a series of actions will be. A well-staged demonstration is particularly effective because it shows proper methods of performance in a realistic manner.

    d. Performance
Performance is one of the most fundamental of all learning techniques or teaching methods. The trainee may be able to tell how a specific operation should be performed but he cannot be sure he knows how to perform the operation until he has done so.
As with all methods, there are certain advantages and disadvantages to each method.

    e. Which Method to Use
Moreover, there are other methods and techniques of teaching. It is difficult to use any method without other methods entering into it. In any learning situation, a combination of methods is usually more effective than any one method alone.

Finally, evaluation must be integrated into the other aspects of the teaching-learning process.

It must be used in the motivation of the trainees; it must be used to assist in developing understanding during the training; and it must be related to employee application of the results of training.

This is distinctly the role of the supervisor.

GLOSSARY OF COMPUTER TERMS

Basic

accessibility
The term accessibility refers to information that can be accessed with fewer or no obstacles for as many people as possible. Developers use accessibility features in websites and software to benefit users with disabilities to use computers through assistive technologies.

artificial intelligence
Artificial intelligence or AI is the ability of a computer to perform tasks related to intelligence and think like humans. This technology can process large amounts of data to recognize patterns and make decisions like humans, as seen in programs like ChatGPT.

API
Also called application programming interface, API is a set of protocols and instructions (written in C++ or JavaScript) to determine how two software components will communicate with each other. It defines the kinds of calls and requests made to locate and retrieve the requested information.

application (app)
An application (often called "app" for short) is a computer program that performs specific functions for an end user or another application (in some cases).

authentication
The process of verification of a user or device before allowing access to the system or resources.

bandwidth
A measurement of the amount of data that can be transmitted over a communications path in a given time. The higher the bandwidth, the greater the volume of data transmitted. It is usually measured in bits per second (bps). Modern networks have speed that is measured in the millions of bits per second (megabits per second, or Mbps) or billions of bits per second (gigabits per second, or Gbps).

blockchain
Blockchain technology is an advanced database mechanism that enables the secure sharing of information. It is also known as distributed ledger technology or DLT. The data is stored in blocks that are lined together in a chain.

boot
Starting up an OS is booting it. If the computer is already running, it is more often called rebooting.

browser
A browser is a program used to browse the web. Some common browsers include Google Chrome, Microsoft Edge, Mozilla Firefox, Brave and Safari.

bug
A bug is a mistake in the design of something, especially software. A really severe bug can cause something to crash.

BYOD
Bring Your Own Device or BYOD is a business policy allowing employees to bring in their personal devices and use them to access company data, e-mail and other resources.

Business Intelligence
Business intelligence or BI is a tool that is used by businesses for data collection, analysis and presentation in a meaningful way to drive the decision-making process.

CAPTCHA
Acronym for Completely Automated Public Turing test to tell Computers and Humans Apart. It is

a test in form of distorted text or images that determines if an online user is really a human or an automated user.
cache
A software or hardware component that temporarily stores data in a computing environment to reduce the data retrieval time for future requests.
chatbot
A chat bot or chatterbox is a computer program that is used for simulating and processing human conversation. It is a form of artificial intelligence (AI) that allows humans to interact with digital devices as if they were communicating with a real person.
chat
Chatting is like e-mail, only it is done instantaneously and can directly involve multiple people at once. Chat is a kind of communication over the Internet that allows real-time transmission of messages between sender and receiver. Chat messages are short to enable the participants to respond quickly.
click
To press a mouse button. When done twice in rapid succession, it is referred to as a double-click.
cloud computing
Refers to storage and access data and programs over the Internet instead of any hard drive. Some common cloud services include Dropbox, iCloud and Google Cloud.
cookie
A piece of data from a website stored within a web browser that a website can retrieve at a later time. It is used throughout a user's session to keep track of usage patterns and preferences.
cursor
A point of attention on the computer screen, often marked with a flashing line or block. Text typed into the computer will usually appear at the cursor.
cybercrime
An illegal activity that involves a network or computer. Some common cybercrimes include identity theft, gaining unauthorized access and network intrusions.
cybersecurity
Measures that are designed to protect information, computer devices or networks from cybercrime.
cyberspace
The world of virtual computers, specifically electronic media, used to facilitate online communication.
data center
A physical facility that is used to house an organization's applications and data. The key components of a data center design include servers, storage systems, firewalls, routers, switches and application-delivery controllers.
database
A database is a collection of data, typically organized to make common retrievals easy and efficient. Some common database programs include Oracle, Sybase, Postgres, Mango DB, Microsoft SQL Server, Redis, Filemaker, Adabas, etc.
decryption
It is the process of converting an encrypted message back to its original form. It is the reverse process of encryption.
desktop
A desktop system is a computer designed to sit in one position on a desk somewhere and not move around. Most general-purpose computers are desktop systems. Calling a system a desktop implies nothing about its platform. Industrial desktop systems are typically called workstations.
directory
Also called "folder," a directory is a collection of files typically created for organizational

purposes. Note that a directory is itself a file, so a directory can generally contain other directories. It differs in this way from a partition.

disk

A disk is a physical object used for storing data. It will not forget its data when it loses power. It is always used in conjunction with a disk drive. Some disks can be removed from their drives, some cannot. Generally it is possible to write new information to a disk in addition to reading data from it, but this is not always the case.

drive

A device for storing and/or retrieving data. Some drives (such as disk drives, zip drives, and tape drives) are typically capable of having new data written to them, but some others (like CD-ROMs or DVD-ROMs) are not. Some drives have random access (like disk drives, zip drives, CD-ROMs, and DVD-ROMs), while others only have sequential access (like tape drives).

e-book

An e-book or electronic book is a digital and non-editable text that is available and displayed on electronic devices (smartphone or tablets). The concept behind an e-book is that it should provide all the functionality of an ordinary book but in a manner that is (overall) less expensive and more environmentally friendly. The actual term e-book is somewhat confusingly used to refer to a variety of things: custom software to play e-book titles, dedicated hardware to play e-book titles, and the e-book titles themselves. Individual e-book titles can be free or commercial (but will always be less expensive than their printed counterparts) and have to be loaded into a player to be read. Players vary wildly in capability level. Basic ones allow simple reading and bookmarking; better ones include various features like hypertext, illustrations, audio, and even limited video. Other optional features allow the user to mark-up sections of text, leave notes, circle or diagram things, highlight passages, program or customize settings, and even use interactive fiction.

email

Email is short for electronic mail. It allows for the transfer of information from one user to others, provided they are hooked up via some sort of network Popular email platforms include Gmail and Yahoo.

encryption

The process of data conversion from readable form into encoded form is called encryption. It is used to hide sensitive information and prevent unauthorized access.

end point

Physical devices that are connected to a computer network such as servers, mobile devices, desktop computers and virtual machines.

end user

An individual who will ultimately use an IT product or service.

file

A file is a unit of (usually named) information stored on a computer.

firewall

A network security device that acts as a barrier to monitor and filter incoming and outgoing network traffic and permits/blocks data packets based on previously established security policies.

firmware

Sort of in-between hardware and software, firmware consists of modifiable programs embedded in hardware. Firmware updates should be treated with care since they can literally destroy the underlying hardware if done improperly. There are also cases where neglecting to apply a firmware update can destroy the underlying hardware, so user beware. Cameras, optical drives, printers, mobile phones, network cards, etc. rely on firmware built into their memory for smooth functioning.

floppy

A once-common type of removable disk. Floppy disks did not hold much data, but most

computers were capable of reading them. They typically held 100 KB to 1.44 MB of data.
format
The manner in which data is stored; its organization. For example, VHS, SVHS, and Beta are three different formats of video tape. They are not 100% compatible with each other, but information can be transferred from one to the other with the proper equipment (but not always without loss; SVHS contains more information than either of the other two). Computer information can be stored in literally hundreds of different formats, and can represent text, sounds, graphics, animations, etc. Computer information can be exchanged via different computer types provided both computers can interpret the format used.
freeware
A type of proprietary software that is available for downloading without charge. Depending on the freeware's copyright, the user may or may not reuse the software.
function keys
On a computer keyboard, the keys that start with an "F" and usually (but not always) found on the top row. They are meant to perform user-defined tasks.
GPS
GPS or Global Positioning System is a radio-based global navigation satellite system that allows the user to determine a location on Earth.
graphics
Anything visually displayed on a computer that is not text.
GUI
A graphical user interface (GUI) is a digital interface through which a user interacts with electronic devices (smartphones, computers) with graphical components such as icons, menus, buttons and other visual indicators. GUI representations are manipulated by mouse, touch screen, finger, stylus, or trackball.
hardware
The physical portion of the computer.
help desk
A help desk is an information and assistance resource that provides technical support for hardware or software. Companies provide help desk support to their customers via a toll-free number, e-mail or website. The goal of a help desk is to help customers troubleshoot issues and guide them to navigate technology properly.
hypertext
A hypertext document is like a text document with the ability to contain pointers to other regions of (possibly other) hypertext documents.
IaaS
Infrastructure as a Service (IaaS) is the most basic cloud-service model that offers computing, storage and networking resources on demand and pay-as-you-go basis.
Internet
The Internet is the world-wide network of computers.
IoT
Internet of Things (IoT) refers to the collective network of connected devices and the technology that facilitates communication between devices and the cloud. IoT includes anything with a sensor that is assigned a unique identifier (UID).
IT infrastructure
Systems that are put in place to facilitate operation and management of IT services and environments. There are two types of IT infrastructure: traditional infrastructure and cloud infrastructure.
keyboard
A keyboard on a computer is almost identical to a keyboard on a typewriter. Computer keyboards will typically have extra keys, however. Some of these keys (common examples include Control, Alt, and Fn) are meant to be used in conjunction with other keys just like shift on

a regular typewriter. Other keys (common examples include Insert, Delete, Home, End, Help, function keys,etc.) are meant to be used independently and often perform editing tasks. Keyboards on different platforms will often look slightly different and have somewhat different collections of keys.

LAN
A local area network (LAN) is a group of connected computing devices that usually share a centralized Internet connection. A LAN may serve 2-3 users in a home or thousands of users in a central office.

language
Computer programs can be written in a variety of different languages. Different languages are optimized for different tasks. Common languages include JavaScript, Python, C#, Rust, Kotlin, Swift, Go and Elixir. Some people classify languages into two categories, higher-level and lower-level. These people would consider assembly language and machine language lower-level languages and all other languages higher-level. In general, higher-level languages can be either interpreted or compiled; many languages allow both, but some are restricted to one or the other. Many people do not consider machine language and assembly language at all when talking about programming languages.

laptop
A laptop is any computer designed for portability with the capability to do most of the same functions as a desktop system. They are battery-powered and typically provide several hours of use between charges. Most laptops run Windows or Apple operating systems, though Google's Chromebook laptop has gained in popularity.

learning management system (LMS)
Software that is developed to create, use, manage, deliver and store online training course content for audience. The primary purpose of an LMS is to simplify the learning process for the organization and keep the knowledge of an audience up to date.

machine learning (ML)
A branch of artificial intelligence (AI) that uses data and algorithms to improve the performance of AI to imitate intelligent human behavior.

malware
Malware, also referred to as malicious software, is a program or file that is designed to disrupt computer systems, networks or servers. Some common types of malware include viruses, worms, Trojan horses, ransomware and spyware.

mail server
A mail server is a dedicated software program that supports electronic mail. It stores incoming mail for distribution to users and forwards outgoing mail. Some common mail servers include Microsoft Exchange, iCloud Mail and Sendmail.

memory
Computer memory is used to temporarily store data. In reality, computer memory is only capable of remembering sequences of zeros and ones, but by utilizing the binary number system it is possible to produce arbitrary rational numbers and through clever formatting all manner of representations of pictures, sounds, and animations. The most common types of memory are RAM, ROM, and flash.

MHz & megahertz
One megahertz is equivalent to 1000 kilohertz, or 1,000,000 hertz. The clock speed of the main processor of many computers is measured in MHz, and is sometimes (quite misleadingly) used to represent the overall speed of a computer. In fact, a computer's speed is based upon many factors, and since MHz only reveals how many clock cycles the main processor has per second (saying nothing about how much is actually accomplished per cycle), it can really only accurately be used to gauge two computers with the same generation and family of processor plus similar configurations of memory, co-processors, and other peripheral hardware.

modem
A modem allows two computers to communicate over ordinary phone lines. It derives its name from modulate / demodulate, the process by which it converts digital computer data back and forth for use with an analog phone line.
monitor
The screen for viewing computer information is called a monitor.
mouse
In computer parlance a mouse can be both the physical object moved around to control a pointer on the screen, and the pointer itself.
multimedia
This originally indicated a capability to work with and integrate various types of things including audio, still graphics, and especially video. Now it is more of a marketing term and has little real meaning.
NC
The term network computer refers to any (usually desktop) computer system that is designed to work as part of a network rather than as a stand-alone machine. This saves money on hardware, software, and maintenance by taking advantage of facilities already available on the network. The term "Internet appliance" is often used interchangeably with NC.
network
A network (as applied to computers) typically means a group of computers working together. It can also refer to the physical wires connecting the computers.
notebook
A notebook is a small laptop with similar price, performance, and battery life.
organizer
An organizer is a tiny computer used primarily to store names, addresses, phone numbers, and date book information. They usually have some ability to exchange information with desktop systems. They are extremely inexpensive but are typically incapable of running any special-purpose applications and are thus of limited use.
OS (Operating System)
The operating system is the program that manages a computer's resources. Commonly used OSs include Ubuntu, Windows, MacOS, Android, and Google ChromeOS.
PaaS
Platform as a Service (PaaS) is a cloud computing model that provides a computing platform including hardware, software, and infrastructure for development, running and management of applications. PaaS frees the developers to install in-house hardware and software to develop or run a new application.
PC
The term personal computer properly refers to any desktop, laptop, or notebook computer system. Its use is inconsistent, though, and some use it to specifically refer Windows-based computers.
PDA
A personal digital assistant is a predecessor of mobile phones and smartphones. It is a small battery-powered computer intended to be carried around by the user rather than left on a desk. It is used to carry out certain functions, including scheduling, organization, translation, etc. PDAs largely became obsolete with the advance and improvement of mobile-phone technology.
phishing
A common type of cyberattack that targets victims through phone calls, email, text messages or other forms of communication. This attack aims to trick the receiver by posing as a trustworthy entity to obtain sensitive information such as credit card details, personally identifiable information and login credentials.
platform
Roughly speaking, a platform represents a computer's family. It is defined by both the processor

type on the hardware side and the OS type on the software side. Computers belonging to different platforms cannot typically run each other's programs (unless the programs are written in a language like Java).

portable
If something is portable it can be easily moved from one type of computer to another. The verb "to port" indicates the moving itself.

printer
A printer is a piece of hardware that will print computer information onto paper.

processor
The processor (also called central processing unit, or CPU) is the part of the computer that actually works with the data and runs the programs. There are two main processor types in common usage today: CISC and RISC. Some computers have more than one processor and are thus called "multiprocessor". This is distinct from multitasking. Advertisers often use megahertz numbers as a means of showing a processor's speed. This is often extremely misleading; megahertz numbers are more or less meaningless when compared across different types of processors.

program
A program is a series of instructions for a computer, telling it what to do or how to behave. The terms "application" and "app" mean almost the same thing (albeit applications generally have GUIs). It is however different from an applet. Program is also the verb that means to create a program, and a programmer is one who programs.

run
Running a program is how it is made to do something. The term "execute" means the same thing.

SaaS
Software as a Service (SaaS) is a cloud-based software delivery model that delivers applications over the Internet. SaaS enables companies to use software on-promise without worrying about installing, renewing and maintaining them.

search engine
A software program or tool that enables the users to search information on the internet. It creates indexes of databases based on titles of files, keywords or full text of files. Google, Baidu and Yahoo are some popular search engines.

SEO
SEO or search engine optimization is the process and practice of improving various aspects of a website to increase its visibility in search engines.

software
The non-physical portion of the computer; the part that exists only as data; the programs. Another term meaning much the same is "code."

spam
Use of electronic messaging systems to send unwanted bulk messages. Different types of spam include phishing emails, email spoofing, tech support scams, malspam, spam calls and spam texts.

spreadsheet
A program used to perform various calculations. It is especially popular for financial applications. Some common spreadsheets include Microsoft Excel and Google Sheets.

Trojan horse
A Trojan horse or Trojan is a type of malware that is designed to disguise itself as legitimate code to perform harmful acts. Once it is inside the network, the attacker can carry out any action that legitimate user could perform such as deleting files, modifying data, exporting files, etc.

troubleshooting
The process of providing technical support that includes identification, planning and resolution of problems, faults or errors within the computer system or software.

user
The operator of a computer.

virtual machine
A virtual machine or VM is a computer resource that is not physical. It uses software instead of a physical computer for running programs and deploying applications. VM software can run operating systems, connect to networks, store data and perform other computational functions. Some popular VM include VMware Workstation, VirtualBox, QEMU, Citrix and VMWare Fusion.

VPN
A virtual private network (VPN) is an encrypted internet connection. A VPN hides actual public IP addresses of the user and tunnels the traffic between user's device and the remote server. The aim of using VPN is to ensure sensitive data is safely transmitted.

WAN
A wide area network or WAN is a type of network that exists over a large geographical area.

Wi-Fi
A wireless technology using radio waves to provide high-speed Internet access.

word processor
A program designed to help with the production of textual documents, like letters and memos. Heavier duty work can be done with a desktop publisher. Some common word processors include Microsoft Word and Google Docs

workstation
A workstation is an individual computer or group of computers that are used by a single user to accomplish professional tasks. Workstations are useful for development and applications that need moderate amount of computing power and high-quality graphics.

www
The World-Wide-Web refers more or less to all the publicly accessible documents on the Internet. It is used quite loosely, and sometimes indicates only HTML files and sometimes FTP and Gopher files, too. It is also sometimes just referred to as "the web".

Reference

The following are past and present elements of computing and computer systems, to be reviewed for reference purposes. In some cases, the element is no longer relevant to modern computing but is important for the study and understanding of previous computing environments.

a11y
Commonly used to abbreviate the word "accessibility." There are eleven letters between the "a" and the "y".

ADA
An object-oriented language at one point popular for military and some academic software.

AIX
The industrial strength OS designed by IBM to run on PowerPC and x86 based machines. It was a variant of UNIX and was meant to provide more power than OS/2.

AJaX
AJaX is a little like DHTML, but it adds asynchronous communication between the browser and Web site via either XML or JSON to achieve performance that often rivals desktop applications.

AltiVec
AltiVec (also called the "Velocity Engine") was a special extension built into some PowerPC CPUs to provide better performance for certain operations, most notably graphics and sound. It was similar to MMX on the x86 CPUs. Like MMX, it required special software for full performance benefits to be realized.

Amiga
A platform originally created and only produced by Commodore and later owned by Gateway 2000 and produced by it and a few smaller companies. It was historically the first multimedia machine and gave the world of computing many innovations. Many music videos were created on Amigas, and a few television series and movies had their special effects generated on Amigas. Also, Amigas were readily synchronized with video cameras, so typically when a computer screen appears on television or in a movie and it is not flickering wildly, it is probably an Amiga in disguise. Many coin-operated arcade games were really Amigas packaged in stand-up boxes.

AmigaOS
The OS used by Amigas. AmigaOS combined the functionality of an OS and a window manager and was fully multitasking. AmigaOS boasted a pretty good selection of games (many arcade games are in fact written on Amigas) but had limited driver support. AmigaOS ran on 68xx, Alpha, and PowerPC based machines.

Apple II
The Apple II computer sold millions of units and is generally considered to have been the first home computer with a 1977 release date. It is based on the 65xx family of processors. The earlier Apple I was only available as a build-it-yourself kit.

AppleScript
A scripting language for Mac OS computers. It is used for basic calculations, text processing and processing complex tasks.

applet
An applet differs from an application in that is not meant to be run stand-alone but rather with the assistance of another program, usually a browser.

Aqua
The default window manager for Mac OS X.

Archie
Archie was a system for searching through FTP archives for particular files. It tends not to be used too much anymore as more general modern search engines are significantly more capable.

ARM
An ARM is a RISC processor invented by Advanced RISC Machines. ARMs are different from most other processors in that they were not designed to maximize speed but rather to maximize speed per power consumed. Thus ARMs found most of their use on hand-held machines and PDAs. A few different OSes run on ARM based machines including Newton OS, JavaOS, Windows CE and Linux. The Cortex-X4 is the fastest ARM CPU ever built.

ASCII
The ASCII character set is the most popular one in common use. People will often refer to a bare text file without complicated embedded format instructions as an ASCII file, and such files can usually be transferred from one computer system to another with relative ease. Unfortunately, there are a few minor variations of it that pop up here and there, and if you receive a text file that seems subtly messed up with punctuation marks altered or upper and lower case reversed, you are probably encountering one of the ASCII variants. It is usually fairly straightforward to translate from one ASCII variant to another, though. The ASCII character set is seven bit while pure binary is usually eight bit, so transferring a binary file through ASCII channels will result in corruption and loss of data. Note also that the ASCII character set is a subset of the Unicode character set.

ASK
A protocol for an infrared communications port on a device. It predates the IrDA compliant infrared communications protocol and is not compatible with it. Many devices with infrared communications support both, but some only support one or the other.

assembly language
Assembly language is essentially machine language that has had some of the numbers

replaced by somewhat easier to remember mnemonics in an attempt to make it more human-readable. The program that converts assembly language to machine language is called an assembler. While assembly language predates FORTRAN, it is not typically what people think of when they discuss computer languages.

authoring system
Any GUIs method of designing new software can be called an authoring system. Any computer language name with the word "visual" in front of it is probably a version of that language built with some authoring system capabilities.

AWK
AWK is an interpreted language developed in 1977 by Aho, Weinberger, & Kernighan. It gets its name from its creators' initials. It was not particularly fast, but it was designed for creating small throwaway programs rather than full-blown applications -- it is designed to make the writing of the program fast, not the program itself. It was quite portable with versions existing for numerous platforms, including a free GNU version. Plus, virtually every version of UNIX in the world came with AWK built-in.

BASIC
The Beginners' All-purpose Symbolic Instruction Code is a computer language developed by Kemeny & Kurtz in 1964.

baud
A measure of communications speed, used typically for modems indicating how many bits per second can be transmitted.

BBS
A bulletin board system was a computer that could be directly connected to via modem and provided various services like e-mail, chatting, newsgroups, and file downloading. BBSs waned in popularity with the rise of Internet access.

BeOS
A lightweight OS available for both PowerPC and x86 based machines. It is often referred to simply as "Be".

beta
A beta version of something is not yet ready for prime time but still possibly useful to related developers and other interested parties. Expect beta software to crash more than properly released software does. Traditionally beta versions (of commercial software) are distributed only to selected testers who are often then given a discount on the proper version after its release in exchange for their testing work. Beta versions of non-commercial software are more often freely available to anyone who has an interest.

binary
There are two meanings for binary in common computer usage. The first is the name of the number system in which there are only zeros and ones. This is important to computers because all computer data is ultimately a series of zeros and ones, and thus can be represented by binary numbers. The second is an offshoot of the first; data that is not meant to be interpreted through a common character set (like ASCII) is typically referred to as binary data. Pure binary data is typically eight bit data, and transferring a binary file through ASCII channels without prior modification will result in corruption and loss of data. Binary data can be turned into ASCII data via uucoding or bcoding.

bit
A bit can either be on or off; one or zero. All computer data can ultimately be reduced to a series of bits. The term is also used as a (very rough) measure of sound quality, color quality, and even processor capability by considering the fact that series of bits can represent binary numbers. For example (without getting too technical), an eight bit image can contain at most 256 distinct colors while a sixteen bit image can contain at most 65,536 distinct colors.

bitmap
A bitmap is a simplistic representation of an image on a computer, simply indicating whether or

not pixels are on or off, and sometimes indicating their color. Often fonts are represented as bitmaps. The term "pixmap" is sometimes used similarly; typically when a distinction is made, pixmap refers to color images and bitmap refers to monochrome images.
blog
Short for web log, a blog is a website or page containing periodic (usually frequent) posts. Blogs are usually syndicated via either some type of RSS or Atom and often supports TrackBacks. It is not uncommon for blogs to function much like newspaper columns. A blogger is someone who writes for and maintains a blog.
boolean
Boolean algebra is the mathematics of base two numbers. Since base two numbers have only two values, zero and one, there is a good analogy between base two numbers and the logical values "true" & "false". In common usage, booleans are therefore considered to be simple logical values like true & false and the operations that relate them, most typically "and", "or" and "not". Since everyone has a basic understanding of the concepts of true & false and basic conjunctions, everyone also has a basic understanding of boolean concepts -- they just may not realize it.
byte
A byte is a grouping of bits. It is typically eight bits, but there are those who use non-standard byte sizes. Bytes are usually measured in large groups, and the term "kilobyte" (often abbreviated as K) means one-thousand twenty-four (1024) bytes; the term "megabyte" (often abbreviated as M) means one-thousand twenty-four (1024) K; the term gigabyte (often abbreviated as G) means one-thousand twenty-four (1024) M; and the term "terabyte" (often abbreviated as T) means one-thousand twenty-four (1024) G. Memory is typically measured in kilobytes or megabytes, and disk space is typically measured in megabytes or gigabytes. Note that the multipliers here are 1024 instead of the more common 1000 as would be used in the metric system. This is to make it easier to work with the binary number system.
bytecode
Sometimes computer languages that are said to be either interpreted or compiled are in fact neither and are more accurately said to be somewhere in between. Such languages are compiled into bytecode which is then interpreted on the target system. Bytecode tends to be binary but will work on any machine with the appropriate runtime environment (or virtual machine) for it.
C
C is one of the most popular computer languages in the world, and quite possibly *the* most popular. It is a compiled language widely supported on many platforms. It tends to be more portable than FORTRAN but less portable than Java; it has been standardized by ANSI as "ANSI C" -- older versions are called either "K&R C" or "Kernighan and Ritchie C" (in honor of C's creators), or sometimes just "classic C". Fast and simple, it can be applied to all manner of general purpose tasks. C compilers are made by several companies, but the free GNU version (gcc) is still considered one of the best. Newer C-like object-oriented languages include both Java and C++.
C#
C# is a compiled object-oriented language based heavily on C++ with some Java features.
C++
C++ is a compiled object-oriented language. Based heavily on C, C++ is nearly as fast and can often be thought of as being just C with added features. It is currently probably the second most popular object-oriented language, but it has the drawback of being fairly complex -- the much simpler but somewhat slower Java is probably the most popular object-oriented language. Note that C++ was developed independently of the somewhat similar Objective-C; it is however related to Objective-C++.
C64/128
The Commodore 64 computer was a massively successful model of computer with estimated

tens of millions units sold. Its big brother, the Commodore 128, was not quite as popular but still sold several million units. Both units sported ROM-based BASIC and used it as a default "OS". The C128 also came with CP/M (it was a not-often-exercized option on the C64). In their later days they were also packaged with GEOS. Both are based on 65xx family processors.

chain
Some computer devices support chaining, the ability to string multiple devices in a sequence plugged into just one computer port. Often, but not always, such a chain will require some sort of terminator to mark the end. For an example, a SCSI scanner may be plugged into a SCSI CD-ROM drive that is plugged into a SCSI hard drive that is in turn plugged into the main computer. For all these components to work properly, the scanner would also have to have a proper terminator in use. Device chaining has been around a long time, and it is interesting to note that C64/128 serial devices supported it from the very beginning.

character set
Since in reality all a computer can store are series of zeros and ones, representing common things like text takes a little work. The solution is to view the series of zeros and ones instead as a sequence of bytes, and map each one to a particular letter, number, or symbol. The full mapping is called a character set. The most popular character set is commonly referred to as ASCII. The second most popular character set is Unicode

COBOL
The Common Business Oriented Language is a language developed back in 1959. While it was relatively portable, it was disliked by many professional programmers simply because COBOL programs tended to be physically longer than equivalent programs written in almost any other language in common use.

compiled
If a program is compiled, its original human-readable source has been converted into a form more easily used by a computer prior to it being run. Such programs will generally run more quickly than interpreted programs, because time was pre-spent in the compilation phase. A program that compiles other programs is called a compiler.

compression
It is often possible to remove redundant information or capitalize on patterns in data to make a file smaller. Usually when a file has been compressed, it cannot be used until it is uncompressed. Image files are common exceptions, though, as many popular image file formats have compression built-in.

cookie
A cookie is a small file that a web page on another machine writes to your personal machine's disk to store various bits of information. Many people strongly detest cookies and the whole idea of them, and most browsers allow the reception of cookies to be disabled or at least selectively disabled. Sites that maintain shopping carts or remember a reader's last position have legitimate uses for cookies. Sites without such functionality that still spew cookies with distant (or worse, non-existent) expiration dates should perhaps be treated with a little caution.

crash
If a bug in a program is severe enough, it can cause that program to crash, or to become inoperable without being restarted. On machines that are not multitasking, the entire machine will crash and have to be rebooted. On machines that are only partially multitasking the entire machine will sometimes crash and have to be rebooted. On machines that are fully multitasking, the machine should never crash and require a reboot.

crippleware
Crippleware is a variant of shareware that will either self-destruct after its trial period or has built-in limitations to its functionality that get removed after its purchase.

CSS
Cascading style sheets are used in conjunction with HTML and XHTML to define the layout of web pages. While CSS is how current web pages declare how they should be displayed, it

tends not to be supported well (if at all) by ancient browsers.
desktop publisher
A program for creating newspapers, magazines, books, etc. Some common desktop publishing programs include Adobe InDesign, Canva, Affinity Publisher and Microsoft Publisher.
DHTML
Dynamic HTML is simply the combined use of both CSS and JavaScript together in the same document; a more extreme form is called AJaX. Note that DHTML is quite different from the similarly named DTML.
dict
A protocol used for looking up definitions across a network (in particular the Internet).
digital camera
A digital camera looks and behaves like a regular camera, except instead of using film, it stores the image it sees in memory as a file for later transfer to a computer. Many digital cameras offer additional storage besides their own internal memory; a few sport some sort of disk but the majority utilize some sort of flash card. Digital cameras were eventually integrated into mobile phones and are now a dominant element of smartphone technology.
DNS
Domain name service is the means by which a name (like www.saugus.net or ftp.saugus.net) gets converted into a real Internet address that points to a particular machine.
DoS
In a denial of service attack, many individual (usually compromised) computers are used to try and simultaneously access the same public resource with the intent of overburdening it so that it will not be able to adequately serve its normal users.
DOS
A disk operating system manages disks and other system resources. Sort of a subset of OSes, sort of an archaic term for the same. MS-DOS is the most popular program currently calling itself a DOS. CP/M was the most popular prior to MS-DOS.
download
To download a file is to copy it from a remote computer to your own. The opposite is upload.
driver
A driver is a piece of software that works with the OS to control a particular piece of hardware, like a printer, scanner or mouse.
DRM
DRM can stand for either Digital Rights Management or Digital Restrictions Management. In either case, DRM is used to place restrictions upon the usage of digital media ranging from software to music to video.
DTML
The Document Template Mark-up Language is a subset of SGML and a superset of HTML used for creating documents that dynamically adapt to external conditions using its own custom tags and a little bit of Python. Note that it is quite different from the similarly named DHTML.
EDBIC
The EDBIC character set is similar to (but less popular than) the ASCII character set in concept, but is significantly different in layout. It tends to be found only on old machines.
embedded
An embedded system is a computer that lives inside another device and acts as a component of that device. For example, cars have an embedded computer under the hood that helps regulate much of their day-to-day operation. An embedded file lives inside another and acts as a portion of that file. This is frequently seen with HTML files having embedded audio files; audio files often embedded in HTML include AU files, MIDI files, SID files, WAV files, AIFF files, and MOD files. Most browsers will ignore these files unless an appropriate plug-in is present.

emulator
An emulator is a program that allows one computer platform to mimic another for the purposes of running its software. Typically (but not always) running a program through an emulator will not be quite as pleasant an experience as running it on the real system.

environment
An environment (sometimes also called a runtime environment) is a collection of external variable items or parameters that a program can access when run. Information about the computer's hardware and the user can often be found in the environment.

extension
Filename extensions allow a grouping of different file types by putting a tag at the end of the name, such as .doc or .pdf.

FAQ
A frequently asked questions file attempts to provide answers for all commonly asked questions related to a given topic.

FireWire
An incredibly fast type of serial port that offers many of the best features of SCSI at a lower price. Faster than most types of parallel port, a single FireWire port is capable of chaining many devices without the need of a terminator. FireWire is similar in many respects to USB but is significantly faster and somewhat more expensive. It is heavily used for connecting audio/video devices to computers, but is also used for connecting storage devices like drives and other assorted devices like printers and scanners.

fixed width
As applied to a font, fixed width means that every character takes up the same amount of space. That is, an "i" will be just as wide as an "m" with empty space being used for padding. The opposite is variable width. The most common fixed width font is Courier.

flash
Flash memory is similar to RAM. It has one significant advantage: it does not lose its contents when power is lost; it has two main disadvantages: it is slower, and it eventually wears out. Flash memory is frequently found in PCMCIA cards.

font
In a simplistic sense, a font can be thought of as the physical description of a character set. While the character set will define what sets of bits map to what letters, numbers, and other symbols, the font will define what each letter, number, and other symbol looks like. Fonts can be either fixed width or variable width and independently, either bitmapped or vectored. The size of the large characters in a font is typically measured in points.

FORTRAN
FORTRAN stands for formula translation and is the oldest computer language in the world. Today languages like C and Java are more popular, but FORTRAN is still heavily used in military software. It is somewhat amusing to note that when FORTRAN was first released back in 1958 its advocates thought that it would mean the end of software bugs. In truth of course by making the creation of more complex software practical, computer languages have merely created new types of software bugs.

FreeBSD
A free variant of Berkeley UNIX available for Alpha and x86 based machines. It was not as popular as Linux.

freeware
Freeware is software that is available for free with no strings attached. The quality is often superb as the authors are also generally users.

FTP
The file transfer protocol is one of the most commonly used methods of copying files across the Internet. It has its origins on UNIX machines, but has been adapted to almost every type of

computer in existence and is built into many browsers. Most FTP programs have two modes of operation, ASCII, and binary. Transmitting an ASCII file via the ASCII mode of operation is more efficient and cleaner. Transmitting a binary file via the ASCII mode of operation will result in a broken binary file. Thus the FTP programs that do not support both modes of operation will typically only do the binary mode, as binary transfers are capable of transferring both kinds of data without corruption.

gateway
A gateway connects otherwise separate computer networks.

GHz & gigahertz
One gigahertz is equivalent to 1000 megahertz, or 1,000,000,000 hertz.

GNOME
The GNU network object model environment was a popular free window manager (and much more -- as its name touts, it is more of a desktop environment) that ran under X-Windows. It was a part of the GNU project.

GNU
GNU stands for GNU's not UNIX and is thus a recursive acronym (and unlike the animal name, the "G" here is pronounced). At any rate, the GNU project is an effort by the Free Software Foundation (FSF) to make all of the traditional UNIX utilities free for whoever wants them.

HP-UX
HP-UX is the version of UNIX designed by Hewlett-Packard to work with their PA-RISC and 68xx based machines.

HTML
The Hypertext Mark-up Language is the language currently most frequently used to express web pages. Every browser has the built-in ability to understand HTML. Some browsers can additionally understand Java and browse FTP areas. HTML is a proper subset of SGML.

http
The hypertext transfer protocol is the native protocol of browsers and is most typically used to transfer HTML formatted files. The secure version is called "https".

Hz & hertz
Hertz means cycles per second, and makes no assumptions about what is cycling. So, for example, if a fluorescent light flickers once per jiffy, it has a 60 Hz flicker. More typical for computers would be a program that runs once per jiffy and thus has a 60 Hz frequency, or larger units of hertz like kHz, MHz, GHz, or THz.

iCalendar
The iCalendar standard refers to the format used to store calendar type information (including events, to-do items, and journal entries) on the Internet. iCalendar data can be found on some World-Wide-Web pages or attached to e-mail messages.

icon
A small graphical display representing an object, action, or modifier of some sort.

Inform
A compiled, object-oriented language optimized for creating interactive fiction.

infrared communications
A device with an infrared port can communicate with other devices at a distance by beaming infrared light signals. Two incompatible protocols are used for infrared communications: IrDA and ASK. Many devices support both.

Instant Messenger
AOL's Instant Messenger was a means of chatting over the Internet in real-time. It allowed both open group discussions and private conversations. Instant Messenger used a different, proprietary protocol from the more standard IRC, and was not supported on as many platforms.

interactive fiction
Interactive fiction (often abbreviated "IF" or "I-F") is a form of literature unique to the computer. While the reader cannot influence the direction of a typical story, the reader plays a more active role in an interactive fiction story and completely controls its direction. Interactive fiction works come in all the sizes and genres available to standard fiction, and in fact are not always even fiction per se (interactive tutorials exist and are slowly becoming more common).

interpreted
If a program is interpreted, its actual human-readable source is read as it is run by the computer. This is generally a slower process than if the program being run has already been compiled.

Intranet
An intranet is a private network. There are many intranets scattered all over the world. Some are connected to the Internet via gateways.

IP
IP is the family of protocols that makes up the Internet.

IRC
Internet relay chat is a means of chatting over the Internet in real-time. It allows both open group discussions and private conversations.

IrDA
The Infrared Data Association (IrDA) is a voluntary organization of various manufacturers working together to ensure that the infrared communications between different computers, printers, digital cameras, remote controls, etc. are all compatible with each other regardless of brand. The term is also often used to designate an IrDA compliant infrared communications port on a device. Informally, a device able to communicate via IrDA compliant infrared is sometimes simply said to "have IrDA". There is also an earlier, incompatible, and usually slower type of infrared communications still in use called ASK.

IRI
An Internationalized Resource Identifier is just a URI with i18n.

IRIX
The variant of UNIX designed by Silicon Graphics, Inc. IRIX machines are known for their graphics capabilities and were initially optimized for multimedia applications.

ISDN
An integrated service digital network line can be simply looked at as a digital phone line. ISDN connections to the Internet can be four times faster than the fastest regular phone connection, and because it is a digital connection a modem is not needed. Any computer hooked up to ISDN will typically require other special equipment in lieu of the modem, however. Also, both phone companies and ISPs charge more for ISDN connections than regular modem connections.

ISP
An Internet service provider is a company that provides Internet support for other entities.

Java
A computer language designed to be both fairly lightweight and extremely portable. It is tightly bound to the web as it is the primary language for web applets. There has also been an OS based on Java for use on small hand-held, embedded, and network computers. It is called JavaOS. Java can be either interpreted or compiled. For web applet use it is almost always interpreted. While its interpreted form tends not to be very fast, its compiled form can often rival languages like C++ for speed. It is important to note however that speed is not Java's primary purpose -- raw speed is considered secondary to portabilty and ease of use.

JavaScript
JavaScript (in spite of its name) has nothing whatsoever to do with Java (in fact, it's arguably more like Newton Script than Java). JavaScript is an interpreted language built into a browser to

provide a relatively simple means of adding interactivity to web pages. It is only supported on a few different browsers, and tends not to work exactly the same on different versions. Thus its use on the Internet is somewhat restricted to fairly simple programs. On intranets where there are usually fewer browser versions in use, JavaScript has been used to implement much more complex and impressive programs.

jiffy
A jiffy is 1/60 of a second. Jiffies are to seconds as seconds are to minutes.

joystick
A joystick is a physical device typically used to control objects on a computer screen. It is frequently used for games and sometimes used in place of a mouse. Today, joysticks are used for gaming, robotics, medical research, virtual reality (VR), and industrial control systems.

JSON
The JSON is used for data interchange between programs, an area in which the ubiquitous XML is not too well-suited. JSON is lightweight and works extremely cleanly with languages including JavaScript, Python, Java, C++, and many others.

JSON-RPC
JSON-RPC is like XML-RPC but is significantly more lightweight since it uses JSON in lieu of XML.

kernel
The very heart of an OS is often called its kernel. It will usually (at minimum) provide some libraries that give programmers access to its various features.

kHz & kilohertz
One kilohertz is equivalent to 1000 hertz. Some older computers have clock speeds measured in kHz.

LDAP
The Lightweight Directory Access Protocol provides a means of sharing address book type of information across an intranet or even across the Internet. Note too that "address book type of information" here is pretty broad; it often includes not just human addresses, but machine addresses, printer configurations, and similar.

library
A selection of routines used by programmers to make computers do particular things.

lightweight
Something that is lightweight will not consume computer resources (such as RAM and disk space) too much and will thus run on less expensive computer systems.

Linux
One of the fastest, most robust, and powerful multitasking OS systems. Linux can be downloaded for free or be purchased for a small service charge. Linux is available for more hardware combinations than any other OS. Fast, reliable, stable, and inexpensive, Linux is popular with ISPs, software developers, and home hobbyists alike.

load
There are two popular meanings for load. The first means to fetch some data or a program from a disk and store it in memory. The second indicates the amount of work a component (especially a processor) is being made to do.

Logo
Logo is an interpreted language designed by Papert in 1966 to be a tool for helping people (especially kids) learn computer programming concepts. In addition to being used for that purpose, it is often used as a language for controlling mechanical robots and other similar devices. Logo interfaces even exist for building block / toy robot sets. Logo uses a special graphics cursor called "the turtle", and Logo is itself sometimes called "Turtle Graphics". Logo is quite portable but not particularly fast. Versions can be found on almost every computer platform in the world. Additionally, some other languages (notably some Pascal versions) provide Logo-

like interfaces for graphics-intensive programming.

lossy

If a process is lossy, it means that a little quality is lost when it is performed. If a format is lossy, it means that putting data into that format (or possibly even manipulating it in that format) will cause some slight loss. Lossy processes and formats are typically used for performance or resource utilization reasons. The opposite of lossy is lossless.

Lua

Lua is a simple interpreted language. It is extremely portable, and free versions exist for most platforms.

Mac OS

Mac OS is the OS used on Macintosh computers. There are two distinctively different versions of it; everything prior to version 10 (sometimes called Mac OS Classic) and everything version 10 or later (called Mac OS X).

Mac OS Classic

The OS created by Apple and originally used by Macs is frequently (albeit slightly incorrectly) referred to as Mac OS Classic (officially Mac OS Classic is this original OS running under the modern Mac OS X in emulation. Mac OS combines the functionality of both an OS and a window manager and is often considered to be the easiest OS to use. It is partially multitasking but will still sometimes crash when dealing with a buggy program. It is probably the second most popular OS, next only to Windows 'XP (although it is quickly losing ground to Mac OS X) and has excellent driver support and boasts a fair selection of games. Mac OS will run on PowerPC and 68xx based machines.

Mac OS X

Mac OS X (originally called Rhapsody) is the industrial strength OS produced by Apple to run on both PowerPC and x86 systems (replacing what is often referred to as Mac OS Classic. Mac OS X is at its heart a variant of UNIX and possesses its underlying power (and the ability to run many of the traditional UNIX tools, including the GNU tools).

machine language

Machine language consists of the raw numbers that can be directly understood by a particular processor. Each processor's machine language will be different from other processors' machine language. Although called "machine language", it is not usually what people think of when talking about computer languages. Machine language dressed up with mnemonics to make it a bit more human-readable is called assembly language.

Macintosh

A Macintosh (or a Mac for short) is a computer system that has Mac OS for its OS. There are a few different companies that have produced Macs, but by far the largest is Apple. The oldest Macs are based on the 68xx processor; somewhat more recent Macs on the PowerPC processor, and current Macs on the x86 processor. The Macintosh was really the first general purpose computer to employ a GUI.

MacTel

An x86 based system running some flavor of Mac OS.

mainframe

A mainframe is any computer larger than a small piece of furniture. A modern mainframe is more powerful than a modern workstation, but more expensive and more difficult to maintain.

MathML

The Math Mark-up Language is a subset of XML used to represent mathematical formulae and equations. Typically it is found embedded within XHTML documents, although as of this writing not all popular browsers support it.

megahertz

A million cycles per second, abbreviated MHz. This is often used misleadingly to indicate processor speed, because while one might expect that a higher number would indicate a faster processor, that logic only holds true within a given type of processors as different types of processors are capable of doing different amounts of work within a cycle. For a current example, either a 200 MHz PowerPC or a 270 MHz SPARC will outperform a 300 MHz Pentium.

middleware
Software designed to sit in between an OS and applications. Common examples are Java and Tcl/Tk.

MIME
The multi-purpose Internet mail extensions specification describes a means of sending non-ASCII data (such as images, sounds, foreign symbols, etc.) through e-mail. It commonly utilizes bcode.

MMX
Multimedia extensions were built into some x86 CPUs to provide better performance for certain operations, most notably graphics and sound. It is similar to AltiVec on the PowerPC CPUs. Like AltiVec, it requires special software for full performance benefits to be realized.

MOB
A movable object is a graphical object that is manipulated separately from the background. These are seen all the time in computer games. When implemented in hardware, MOBs are sometimes called sprites.

Modula-2 & Modula-3
Modula-2 is a procedural language based on Pascal by its original author in around the 1977 1979 time period. Modula-3 is an intended successor that adds support for object-oriented constructs (among other things). Modula-2 can be either compiled or interpreted, while Modula-3 tends to be just a compiled language.

MOTD
A message of the day. Many computers (particularly more capable ones) are configured to display a MOTD when accessed remotely.

MS-DOS
The DOS produced by Microsoft. Early versions of it bear striking similarities to the earlier CP/M, but it utilizes simpler commands. It provides only a CLI, but either OS/2, Windows 3.1, Windows '95, Windows '98, Windows ME, or GEOS may be run on top of it to provide a GUI. It only runs on x86 based machines.

MS-Windows
MS-Windows is the name collectively given to several somewhat incompatible OSes all produced by Microsoft. The latest Windows update is Windows 11, version 23H2.

MUD
A multi-user dimension (also sometimes called multi-user dungeon, but in either case abbreviated to "MUD") is sort of a combination between the online chatting abilities provided by something like IRC and a role-playing game. A MUD built with object oriented principles in mind is called a "Multi-user dimension object-oriented", or MOO. Yet another variant is called a "multi-user shell", or MUSH. Still other variants are called multi-user role-playing environments (MURPE) and multi-user environments (MUSE). There are probably more. In all cases the differences will be mostly academic to the regular user, as the same software is used to connect to all of them. Software to connect to MUDs can be found for most platforms, and there are even Java based ones that can run from within a browser.

multitasking
Some OSes have built into them the ability to do several things at once. This is called multitasking, and has been in use since the late sixties / early seventies. Since this ability is built into the software, the overall system will be slower running two things at once than it will be running just one thing. A system may have more than one processor built into it though, and such a system will be capable of running multiple things at once with less of a performance hit.

nagware
Nagware is a variant of shareware that will frequently remind its users to register.

NetBSD
A free variant of Berkeley UNIX available for Alpha, x86, 68xx, PA-RISC, SPARC, PowerPC, ARM, and many other types of machines. Its emphasis is on portability.
newbie
A newbie is a novice to the online world or computers in general.
news
Usenet news can generally be thought of as public e-mail as that is generally the way it behaves. In reality, it is implemented by different software and is often accessed by different programs. Different newsgroups adhere to different topics, and some are "moderated", meaning that humans will try to manually remove off-topic posts, especially spam. Most established newsgroups have a FAQ, and people are strongly encouraged to read the FAQ prior to posting.
Newton
Although Newton is officially the name of the lightweight OS developed by Apple to run on its MessagePad line of PDAs, it is often used to mean the MessagePads (and compatible PDAs) themselves and thus the term "Newton OS" is often used for clarity. The Newton OS is remarkably powerful; it is fully multitasking in spite of the fact that it was designed for small machines. It is optimized for hand-held use, but will readily transfer data to all manner of desktop machines. Historically it was the first PDA. Recently Apple announced that it will discontinue further development of the Newton platform, but will instead work to base future hand-held devices on either Mac OS or Mac OS X with some effort dedicated to making the new devices capable of running current Newton programs.
Newton book
Newton books provide all the functionality of ordinary books but add searching and hypertext capabilities. The format was invented for the Newton to provide a means of making volumes of data portable, and is particularly popular in the medical community as most medical references are available as Newton books and carrying around a one pound Newton is preferable to carrying around twenty pounds of books, especially when it comes to looking up something. In addition to medical books, numerous references, most of the classics, and many contemporary works of fiction are available as Newton books. Most fiction is available for free, most references cost money. Newton books are somewhat more capable than the similar Palm DOC; both are specific types of e-books.
nybble
A nybble is half a byte, or four bits. It is a case of computer whimsy; it only stands to reason that a small byte should be called a nybble. Some authors spell it with an "i" instead of the "y", but the "y" is the original form.
object-oriented
The term "object-oriented" applies to a philosophy of software creation. Often this philosophy is referred to as object-oriented design (sometimes abbreviated as OOD), and programs written with it in mind are referred to as object-oriented programs (often abbreviated OOP). Programming languages designed to help facilitate it are called object-oriented languages (sometimes abbreviated as OOL) and databases built with it in mind are called object-oriented databases (sometimes abbreviated as OODB or less fortunately OOD). The general notion is that an object-oriented approach to creating software starts with modeling the real-world problems trying to be solved in familiar real-world ways, and carries the analogy all the way down to structure of the program. This is of course a great over-simplification. Numerous object-oriented programming languages exist including: Java, C++, Modula-2, Newton Script, and ADA.
Objective-C & ObjC
Objective-C (often called "ObjC" for short) is a compiled object-oriented language. Based heavily on C, Objective-C is nearly as fast and can often be thought of as being just C with added features. Note that it was developed independently of C++; its object-oriented extensions are more in the style of Smalltalk. It is however related to Objective-C++.
Objective-C++ & ObjC++

Objective-C++ (often called "ObjC++" for short) is a curious hybrid of Objective-C and C++, allowing the syntax of both to coexist in the same source files.

office suite

An office suite is a collection of programs including at minimum a word processor, spreadsheet, drawing program, and minimal database program. Some popular office suites include Google Workspace, Microsoft 365, iWork, LibreOffice, Polaris Office and OpenOffice.

open source

Open source software goes one step beyond freeware. Not only does it provide the software for free, it provides the original source code used to create the software. Thus, curious users can poke around with it to see how it works, and advanced users can modify it to make it work better for them. By its nature, open source software is pretty well immune to all types of computer virus.

OpenBSD

A free variant of Berkeley UNIX available for Alpha, x86, 68xx, PA-RISC, SPARC, and PowerPC based machines. Its emphasis is on security.

OpenDocument & ODF

OpenDocument (or ODF for short) is the suite of open, XML-based office suite application formats defined by the OASIS consortium. It defines a platform-neutral, non-proprietary way of storing documents.

OpenGL

A low-level 3D graphics library with an emphasis on speed developed by SGI.

OS/2

OS/2 is the OS designed by IBM to run on x86 based machines. It is semi-compatible with MS-Windows. IBM's more industrial strength OS is called AIX.

Palm Pilot

The Palm Pilot (also called both just Palm and just Pilot, officially now just Palm) was the most popular PDA in use. It was one of the least capable PDAs but also one of the smallest and least expensive. While not as full-featured as many of the other PDAs (such as the Newton), it performed what features it did have quite well.

parallel

Loosely speaking, parallel implies a situation where multiple things can be done simultaneously, like having multiple check-out lines each serving people all at once. Parallel connections are by their nature more expensive than serial ones, but usually faster. Also, in a related use of the word, often multitasking computers are said to be capable of running multiple programs in parallel.

partition

Sometimes due to hardware limitations, disks have to be divided into smaller pieces. These pieces are called partitions.

Pascal

Named after the mathematician Blaise Pascal, Pascal is a language designed by Niklaus Wirth originally in 1968 (and heavily revised in 1972) mostly for purposes of education and training people how to write computer programs. It is a typically compiled language but is still usually slower than C or FORTRAN. Wirth also created a more powerful object-oriented Pascal-like language called Modula-2.

PC-DOS

The DOS produced by IBM designed to work like MS-DOS. Early versions of it bear striking similarities to the earlier CP/M, but it utilizes simpler commands. It provides only a CLI, but either Windows 3.1 or GEOS may be run on top of it to provide a GUI. It only runs on x86 based machines.

PCMCIA

The Personal Computer Memory Card International Association is a standards body that concern themselves with PC Card technology. Often the PC Cards themselves are referred

to as "PCMCIA cards". Frequently flash memory can be found in PC card form.
Perl
Perl is an interpreted language extremely popular for web applications.
PET
The Commodore PET (Personal Electronic Transactor) is an early (circa 1977-1980, around the same time as the Apple][) home computer featuring a ROM-based BASIC developed by Microsoft which it uses as a default "OS". It is based on the 65xx family of processors and is the precursor to the VIC-20.
PHP
Named with a recursive acronym (PHP: Hypertext Preprocessor), PHP provides a means of creating web pages that dynamically modify themselves on the fly.
ping
Ping is a protocol designed to check across a network to see if a particular computer is "alive" or not. Computers that recognize the ping will report back their status. Computers that are down will not report back anything at all.
pixel
The smallest distinct point on a computer display is called a pixel.
plug-in
A plug-in is a piece of software designed not to run on its own but rather work in cooperation with a separate application to increase that application's abilities.
point
There are two common meanings for this word. The first is in the geometric sense; a position in space without size. Of course as applied to computers it must take up some space in practice (even if not in theory) and it is thus sometimes synonymous with pixel. The other meaning is related most typically to fonts and regards size. The exact meaning of it in this sense will unfortunately vary somewhat from person to person, but will often mean 1/72 of an inch. Even when it does not exactly mean 1/72 of an inch, larger point sizes always indicate larger fonts.
PowerPC
The PowerPC is a RISC processor developed in a collaborative effort between IBM, Apple, and Motorola. It is currently produced by a few different companies, of course including its original developers. A few different OSes run on PowerPC based machines, including Mac OS, AIX, Solaris, Windows NT, Linux, Mac OS X, BeOS, and AmigaOS. At any given time, the fastest processor in the world is usually either a PowerPC or an Alpha, but sometimes SPARCs and PA-RISCs make the list, too.
proprietary
This simply means to be supplied by only one vendor. It is commonly misused. Currently, most processors are non-proprietary, some systems are non-proprietary, and every OS (except for arguably Linux) is proprietary.
protocol
A protocol is a means of communication used between computers. As long as both computers recognize the same protocol, they can communicate without too much difficulty over the same network or even via a simple direct modem connection regardless whether or not they are themselves of the same type. This means that WinTel boxes, Macs, Amigas, UNIX machines, etc., can all talk with one another provided they agree on a common protocol first.
queue
A queue is a waiting list of things to be processed. Many computers provide printing queues, for example. If something is being printed and the user requests that another item be printed, the second item will sit in the printer queue until the first item finishes printing at which point it will be removed from the queue and get printed itself.
RAM
Random access memory is the short-term memory of a computer. Any information stored in

RAM will be lost if power goes out, but the computer can read from RAM far more quickly than from a drive.

random access
Also called "dynamic access" this indicates that data can be selected without having to skip over earlier data first. This is the way that a CD, record, laserdisc, or DVD will behave -- it is easy to selectively play a particular track without having to fast forward through earlier tracks. The other common behavior is called sequential access.

RDF
The Resource Description Framework is built upon an XML base and provides a more modern means of accessing data from Internet resources. It can provide metadata (including annotations) for web pages making (among other things) searching more capable. It is also being used to refashion some existing formats like RSS and iCalendar; in the former case it is already in place (at least for newer RSS versions), but it is still experimental in the latter case.

real-time
Something that happens in real-time will keep up with the events around it and never give any sort of "please wait" message.

Rexx
The Restructured Extended Executor is an interpreted language designed primarily to be embedded in other applications in order to make them consistently programmable, but also to be easy to learn and understand.

RISC
Reduced instruction set computing is one of the two main types of processor design in use today, the other being CISC. The fastest processors in the world today are all RISC designs. There are several popular RISC processors, including Alphas, ARMs, PA-RISCs, PowerPCs, and SPARCs.

robot
A robot (or 'bot for short) in the computer sense is a program designed to automate some task, often just sending messages or collecting information. A spider is a type of robot designed to traverse the web performing some task (usually collecting data).

robust
The adjective robust is used to describe programs that are better designed, have fewer bugs, and are less likely to crash.

ROM
Read-only memory is similar to RAM only cannot be altered and does not lose its contents when power is removed.

RSS
RSS stands for either Rich Site Summary, Really Simple Syndication, or **RDF** Site Summary, depending upon whom you ask. The general idea is that it can provide brief summaries of articles that appear in full on a web site. It is well-formed XML, and newer versions are even more specifically well-formed RDF.

Ruby
Ruby is an interpreted, object-oriented language. Ruby was fairly heavily influenced by Perl, so people familiar with that language can typically transition to Ruby easily.

scanner
A scanner is a piece of hardware that will examine a picture and produce a computer file that represents what it sees. A digital camera is a related device. Each has its own limitations.

script
A script is a series of OS commands. The term "batch file" means much the same thing, but is a bit dated. Typically the same sort of situations in which one would say DOS instead of OS, it would also be appropriate to say batch file instead of script. Scripts can be run like programs, but tend to perform simpler tasks. When a script is run, it is always interpreted.

SCSI
Loosely speaking, a disk format sometimes used by MS-Windows, Mac OS, AmigaOS, and (almost always) UNIX. Generally SCSI is superior (but more expensive) to IDE, but it varies somewhat with system load and the individual SCSI and IDE components themselves. The quick rundown is that: SCSI-I and SCSI-II will almost always outperform IDE; EIDE will almost always outperform SCSI-I and SCSI-II; SCSI-III and UltraSCSI will almost always outperform EIDE; and heavy system loads give an advantage to SCSI. Note that although loosely speaking it is just a format difference, it is deep down a hardware difference.

sequential access
This indicates that data cannot be selected without having to skip over earlier data first. This is the way that a cassette or video tape will behave. The other common behavior is called random access.

serial
Loosely speaking, serial implies something that has to be done linearly, one at a time, like people being served in a single check-out line. Serial connections are by their nature less expensive than parallel connections (including things like SCSI) but are typically slower.

server
A server is a computer designed to provide various services for an entire network. It is typically either a workstation or a mainframe because it will usually be expected to handle far greater loads than ordinary desktop systems. The load placed on servers also necessitates that they utilize robust OSes, as a crash on a system that is currently being used by many people is far worse than a crash on a system that is only being used by one person.

SGML
The Standard Generalized Mark-up Language provides an extremely generalized level of mark-up. More common mark-up languages like HTML and XML are actually just popular subsets of SGML.

shareware
Shareware is software made for profit that allows a trial period before purchase. Typically shareware can be freely downloaded, used for a period of weeks (or sometimes even months), and either purchased or discarded after it has been learned whether or not it will satisfy the user's needs.

shell
A CLI designed to simplify complex OS commands. Some OSes (like AmigaOS, the Hurd, and UNIX) have built-in support to make the concurrent use of multiple shells easy. Common shells include the Korn Shell (ksh), the Bourne Shell (sh or bsh), the Bourne-Again Shell, (bash or bsh), the C-Shell (csh), etc.

SIMM
A physical component used to add RAM to a computer. Similar to, but incompatible with, DIMMs.

Smalltalk
Smalltalk is an efficient language for writing computer programs. Historically it is one of the first object-oriented languages, and is not only used today in its pure form but shows its influence in other languages like Objective-C.

spam
Generally spam is unwanted, unrequested e-mail or some other form of contact. It is typically sent out in bulk to huge address lists that were automatically generated by various robots endlessly searching the Internet and newsgroups for things that resemble e-mail addresses.

SPARC
The SPARC was a RISC processor developed by Sun.

sprite
The term sprite originally referred to a small MOB, usually implemented in hardware. Lately it

is also being used to refer to a single image used piecemeal within a Web site in order to avoid incurring the time penalty of downloading multiple files.
SQL
SQL (pronounced Sequel) is an interpreted language specially designed for database access. It is supported by virtually every major modern database system.
SVG
Scalable Vector Graphics data is an XML file that is used to hold graphical data that can be resized without loss of quality. SVG data can be kept in its own file, or even embedded within a web page (although not all browsers are capable of displaying such data).
Tonic
The Tool Command Language is a portable interpreted computer language designed to be easy to use. Tk is a GUI toolkit for Tcl. Tcl is a fairly popular language for both integrating existing applications and for creating Web applets (note that applets written in Tcl are often called Tcklets). Tcl/Tk is available for free for most platforms, and plug-ins are available to enable many browsers to play Tcklets.
TCP/IP
TCP/IP is a protocol for computer networks. The Internet is largely built on top of TCP/IP (it is the more reliable of the two primary Internet Protocols -- TCP stands for Transmission Control Protocol).
terminator
A terminator is a dedicated device used to mark the end of a device chain (as is most typically found with SCSI devices). If such a chain is not properly terminated, weird results can occur.
TEX
TEX (pronounced "tek") is a freely available, industrial strength typesetting program that can be run on many different platforms. These qualities make it exceptionally popular in schools, and frequently software developed at a university will have its documentation in TEX format. TEX is not limited to educational use, though; many professional books were typeset with TEX. TEX's primary drawback is that it can be quite difficult to set up initially.
THz & terahertz
One terahertz is equivalent to 1000 gigahertz.
TrackBack
TrackBacks essentially provide a means whereby different web sites can post messages to one another not just to inform each other about citations, but also to alert one another of related resources. Typically, a blog may display quotations from another blog through the use of TrackBacks.
UDP/IP
UDP/IP is a protocol for computer networks. It is the faster of the two primary Internet Protocols. UDP stands for User Datagram Protocol.
Unicode
The Unicode character set is a superset of the ASCII character set with provisions made for handling international symbols and characters from other languages. Unicode is sixteen bit, so takes up roughly twice the space as simple ASCII, but is correspondingly more flexible.
UNIX
UNIX is a family of OSes, each being made by a different company or organization but all offering a very similar look and feel. It cannot quite be considered non-proprietary, however, as the differences between different vendor's versions can be significant (it is still generally possible to switch from one vendor's UNIX to another without too much effort; today the differences between different UNIXes are similar to the differences between the different MS-Windows; historically there were two different UNIX camps, Berkeley / BSD and AT&T / System V, but the assorted vendors have worked together to minimize the differences). The free variant Linux is one of the closest things to a current, non-proprietary OS; its development is controlled by a non-profit organization and its distribution is provided by several companies. UNIX is powerful; it is

fully multitasking and can do pretty much anything that any OS can do (look to the Hurd if you need a more powerful OS). With power comes complexity, however, and UNIX tends not to be overly friendly to beginners (although those who think UNIX is difficult or cryptic apparently have not used CP/M). Window managers are available for UNIX (running under X-Windows) and once properly configured common operations will be almost as simple on a UNIX machine as on a Mac. Out of all the OSes in current use, UNIX has the greatest range of hardware support. It will run on machines built around many different processors.

upload
To upload a file is to copy it from your computer to a remote computer. The opposite is download.

UPS
An uninterrupted power supply uses heavy duty batteries to help smooth out its input power source.

URI
A Uniform Resource Identifier is basically just a unique address for almost any type of resource. It is similar to but more general than a URL; in fact, it may also be a URN.

URL
A Uniform Resource Locator is basically just an address for a file that can be given to a browser. It starts with a protocol type (such as http, ftp, or gopher) and is followed by a colon, machine name, and file name in UNIX style. Optionally an octothorpe character "#" and and arguments will follow the file name; this can be used to further define position within a page and perform a few other tricks. Similar to but less general than a URI.

URN
A Uniform Resource Name is basically just a unique address for almost any type of resource unlike a URL it will probably not resolve with a browser.

USB
A really fast type of serial port that offers many of the best features of SCSI without the price. Faster than many types of parallel port, a single USB port is capable of chaining many devices without the need of a terminator. USB is much slower (but somewhat less expensive) than FireWire.

uucode
The point of uucode is to allow 8-bit binary data to be transferred through the more common 7-bit ASCII channels (most especially e-mail). The facilities for dealing with uucoded files exist for many different machine types, and the most common programs are called "uuencode" for encoding the original binary file into a 7-bit file and "uudecode" for restoring the original binary file from the encoded one. Sometimes different uuencode and uudecode programs will work in subtly different manners causing annoying compatibility problems. Bcode was invented to provide the same service as uucode but to maintain a tighter standard.

variable width
As applied to a font, variable width means that different characters will have different widths as appropriate. For example, an "i" will take up much less space than an "m". The opposite of variable width is fixed width. The terms "proportional width" and "proportionally spaced" mean the same thing as variable width. Some common variable width fonts include Times, Helvetica, and Bookman.

vector
This term has two common meanings. The first is in the geometric sense: a vector defines a direction and magnitude. The second concerns the formatting of fonts and images. If a font is a vector font or an image is a vector image, it is defined as lines of relative size and direction rather than as collections of pixels (the method used in bitmapped fonts and images). This makes it easier to change the size of the font or image, but puts a bigger load on the device that has to display the font or image. The term "outline font" means the same thing as vector font.

VIC-20
The Commodore VIC-20 computer sold millions of units and is generally considered to have been the first affordable home computer. It features a ROM-based BASIC and uses it as a default "OS". It is based on the 65xx family of processors. VIC (in case you are wondering) can stand for either video interface **c** or video interface computer. The VIC-20 is the precursor to the C64/128.

virtual machine
A virtual machine is a machine completely defined and implemented in software rather than hardware. It is often referred to as a "runtime environment"; code compiled for such a machine is typically called bytecode.

virtual memory
This is a scheme by which disk space is made to substitute for the more expensive RAM space. Using it will often enable a comptuer to do things it could not do without it, but it will also often result in an overall slowing down of the system. The concept of swap space is very similar.

virtual reality
Virtual reality (often called VR for short) is generally speaking an attempt to provide more natural, human interfaces to software. It can be as simple as a pseudo 3D interface or as elaborate as an isolated room in which the computer can control the user's senses of vision, hearing, and even smell and touch.

virus
A virus is a program that will seek to duplicate itself in memory and on disks, but in a subtle way that will not immediately be noticed. A computer on the same network as an infected computer or that uses an infected disk (even a floppy) or that downloads and runs an infected program can itself become infected. A virus can only spread to computers of the same platform. For example, on a network consisting of a WinTel box, a Mac, and a Linux box, if one machine acquires a virus the other two will probably still be safe.

VMS
The industrial strength OS that runs on VAXen.

VoIP
VoIP means "Voice over IP" and it is quite simply a way of utilizing the Internet (or even in some cases intranets) for telephone conversations. The primary motivations for doing so are cost and convenience as VoIP is significantly less expensive than typical telephone long distance packages, plus one high speed Internet connection can serve for multiple phone lines.

VRML
A Virtual Reality Modeling Language file is used to represent VR objects. It has essentially been superceded by X3D.

W3C
The World Wide Web Consortium (usually abbreviated W3C) is a non-profit, advisory body that makes suggestions on the future direction of the World Wide Web, HTML, CSS, and browsers.

Waba
An extremely lightweight subset of Java optimized for use on PDAs.

WebDAV
WebDAV stands for Web-based Distributed Authoring and Versioning, and is designed to provide a way of editing Web-based resources in place. It serves as a more modern (and often more secure) replacement for FTP in many cases.

WebTV
A1NebTV box hooks up to an ordinary television set and displays web pages. It will not display them as well as a dedicated computer.

window manager
A window manager is a program that acts as a graphical go-between for a user and an OS. It provides a GUI for the OS. Some OSes incorporate the window manager into their own internal code, but many do not for reasons of efficiency. Some OSes partially make the division. Some

common true window managers include CDE (Common Desktop Environment), GNOME, KDE, Aqua, OpenWindows, Motif, FVWM, Sugar, and Enlightenment. Some common hybrid window managers with OS extensions include Windows ME, Windows 98, Windows 95, Windows 3.1, OS/2 and GEOS.

WinTel
An x86 based system running some flavor of MS-Windows.

workstation
Depending upon whom you ask, a workstation is either an industrial strength desktop computer or its own category above the desktops. Workstations typically have some flavor of UNIX for their OS, but there has been a recent trend to call high-end Windows NT and Windows 2000 machines workstations, too.

WYSIWYG
What you see is what you get; an adjective applied to a program that attempts to exactly represent printed output on the screen. Related to WYSIWYM but quite different.

WYSIWYM
What you see is what you mean; an adjective applied to a program that does not attempt to exactly represent printed output on the screen, but rather defines how things are used and so will adapt to different paper sizes, etc. Related to WYSIWYG but quite different.

X-Face
X-Faces are small monochrome images embedded in headers for both provides a e-mail and news messages. Better mail and news applications will display them (sometimes automatically, sometimes only per request).

X-Windows
X-Windows provides a GUI for most UNIX systems, but can also be found as an add-on library for other computers. Numerous window managers run on top of it. It is often just called "X".

X3D
Extensible **3D** Graphics data is an XML file that is used to hold three-dimensional graphical data. It is the successor to VRML.

x86
The x86 series of processors includes the Pentium, Pentium Pro, Pentium II, Pentium III, Celeron, and Athlon as well as the 786, 686, 586, 486, 386, 286, 8086, 8088, etc. It is an exceptionally popular design (by far the most popular CISC series) in spite of the fact that even its fastest model is significantly slower than the assorted RISC processors. Many different OSes run on machines built around x86 processors, including MS-DOS, Windows 3.1, Windows '95, Windows '98, Windows ME, Windows NT, Windows 2000, Windows CE, Windows XP, GEOS, Linux, Solaris, OpenBSD, NetBSD, FreeBSD, Mac OS X, OS/2, BeOS, CP/M, etc. A couple different companies produce x86 processors, but the bulk of them are produced by Intel. It is expected that this processor will eventually be completely replaced by the Merced, but the Merced development schedule is somewhat behind. Also, it should be noted that the Pentium III processor has stirred some controversy by including a "fingerprint" that will enable individual computer usage of web pages etc. to be accurately tracked.

XBL
An XML Binding Language document is used to associate executable content with an XML tag. It is itself an XML file, and is used most frequently (although not exclusively) in conjunction with XUL.

XHTML
The Extensible Hypertext Mark-up Language is essentially a cleaner, stricter version of HTML. It is a proper subset of XML.

XML
The Extensible Mark-up Language is a subset of SGML and a superset of XHTML. It is used for numerous things including (among many others) RSS and RDF.

XML-RPC
XML-RPC provides a fairly lightweight means by which one computer can execute a program on a co-operating machine across a network like the Internet. It is based on XML and is used for everything from fetching stock quotes to checking weather forcasts.
XO
The energy-efficient, kid-friendly laptop produced by the OLPC project. It runs Sugar for its window manager and Linux for its OS. It sports numerous built-in features like wireless networking, a video camera & microphone, a few USB ports, and audio in/out jacks. It comes with several educational applications (which it refers to as "Activities"), most of which are written in Python.
XSL
The Extensible Stylesheet Language is like CSS for XML. It provides a means of describing how an XML resource should be displayed.
XSLT
XSL Transformations are used to transform one type of XML into another. It is a component of XSL that can be (and often is) used independently.
XUL
An XML User-Interface Language document is used to define a user interface for an application using XML to specify the individual controls as well as the overall layout.
Z-Machine
A virtual machine optimized for running interactive fiction, interactive tutorials, and other interactive things of a primarily textual nature. Z-Machines have been ported to almost every platform in use today. Z-machine bytecode is usually called Z-code. The Glulx virtual machine is of the same idea but somewhat more modern in concept.
zip
There are three common zips in the computer world that are completely different from one another. One is a type of removable removable disk slightly larger (physically) and vastly larger (capacity) than a floppy. The second is a group of programs used for running interactive fiction. The third is a group of programs used for compression.